D1279138

Books by Eric Hammel

ISLANDS OF HELL

THE U.S. MARINES IN THE WESTERN PACIFIC
1944–1945

Eric Hammel

ZENITH PRESS

First published in 2010 by Zenith Press, an imprint of MBI Publishing Company,
400 First Avenue North, Suite 300, Minneapolis, MN 55401 USA

Zenith Press titles are also available at discounts in bulk quantity for industrial or sales-
promotional use. For details write to Special Sales Manager at MBI Publishing Company,
400 First Avenue North, Suite 300, Minneapolis, MN 55401 USA.

To find out more about our books, join us online at www.zenithpress.com.

Printed in China

Library of Congress Cataloging-in-Publication Data

Hammel, Eric M.
Islands of hell : the U.S. Marines in the Western Pacific, 1944–1945 / Eric Hammel.
   p. cm.
  Includes bibliographical references and index.
  ISBN 978-0-7603-3779-0 (hb w/ jkt)
  1. United States. Marine Corps—History—World War, 1939–1945. 2. World War, 1939–
1945—Campaigns—Pacific Area. I. Title.
  D769.369.H35 2010
  940.54'5973—dc22
                     2009030268

Credits:
Maps by Philip Schwartzberg, Meridian Mapping
On the cover, frontispiece, title page, contents page, and back cover: *Official USMC Photos*

Epigraph from an anonymous poem found on a grave marker on Guadalcanal.

This book is dedicated in loving memory to my father

Fred L. Hammel

1921–2001

a German Holocaust refugee who was wounded in action on Okinawa

while serving as a U.S. Army front-line combat medic with the

2d Battalion, 184th Infantry Regiment, 7th Infantry Division

And when he gets to Heaven,
To Saint Peter he will tell,
"One more Marine reporting, sir.
I've served my time in Hell." Eph. 2:8-10

CONTENTS

MAPS

AUTHOR'S NOTE

DURING THE FIRST FOURTEEN MONTHS of the Pacific War, the Marine Corps devoted few resources to documenting the war on film. Very few photographers were deployed to the Pacific, and they were neither trained nor often called upon to act as *combat* photographers. That worldview, the name, and the training to go with it did not really emerge in the field until late 1943, at Bougainville, Cape Gloucester, and Tarawa. Those campaigns have been covered in my *U.S. Marines in World War II* series, and Tarawa has been covered in greater detail in *Bloody Tarawa,* which I wrote years ago with the late John E. Lane, a Tarawa combat veteran. The large, singularly stunning body of combat photographs to emerge from the struggle for Iwo Jima, covered in Part II of the current volume, is also liberally sampled in my in-depth single-volume 2006 study *Iwo Jima: Portrait of a Battle.*

The photographic record that started so slowly and unevenly at Guadalcanal and on through the central Solomons perked up in November 1943, at both Bougainville and Tarawa, as more and better-organized photographers with a better idea about what to photograph moved into battle with Marine combat units. The photographic record is much larger and visibly mounts in intensity as one follows the Marines across the wide Pacific. The photos are of better quality, more immediate, more sympathetic toward the combat Marines who have to assault the beaches, brave the fire, take the hills, comb the valleys and forests, and reduce all manner of Japanese defensive schemes that mark the long, long road to victory. The photos become more knowing and more insightful as the photographers begin to share the day-to-day, moment-by-moment, life-and-death struggles their combatant comrades are thrown into. Indeed, as the photographers got more battle experience under their own belts, they became more hardbitten—more fatalistic and less cautious, yet more willing to come to grips with the many faces of war that express themselves all around them as other young men fought and died on the shared battlefield, in the shared state of privation. That will be evident as you encounter the photographic record in this volume.

ACKNOWLEDGMENTS

FOR PRICELESS HELP in accessing and scanning photos in official collections, and for being there with good advice and information, I thank Theresa M. Roy and Holly Reed at the Still Pictures branch of the National Archives and Records Administration; Mike Miller, Patricia Mullen, and Sue Dillon at the Marine Corps University Archive at Quantico, Virginia; Colonel Walt Ford and Nancy Hoffman at *Leatherneck Magazine;* and Colonel Dick Camp and Lena Kaljot at the Marine Corps Historical Division.

PROLOGUE

★ ★ ★ ★ ★

ON AUGUST 7, 1942, eight months to the day following the December 7, 1941, Japanese attack on Pearl Harbor, the United States struck back against the empire's Pacific juggernaut with an ill-planned amphibious assault at Guadalcanal by the undertrained 1st Marine Division. Although the Anglo-American war plan called for the defeat of Germany foremost, news that a Japanese airfield was under construction in the Eastern Solomon Islands was too provocative to ignore; aircraft that would soon operate from the new airfield would threaten the vital sea lanes connecting the U.S. mainland to the principal Allied Pacific base and war depot in Australia. The stakes were high for the first major Allied offensive in the Pacific, and the 1st Marine Division's four-and-a-half-month stand on Guadalcanal was a cliffhanger from start to finish, but the Marines defeated the Japanese army in one close-run action after another.

The American victory at Guadalcanal was followed by the commitment of several Marine battalions to the U.S. Army–run New Georgia Campaign, and Marine Corps aviation came into its own during the year-long Allied advance from Guadalcanal through the Central Solomon Islands. The 3d Marine Division invaded Bougainville on November 1, 1943, and the 1st Marine Division went into action again in western New Britain in late December 1943. Also by late December, Marine Air had become the preponderant force in the air assault on Japan's regional fortress at Rabaul, in eastern New Britain. Meanwhile, the Guadalcanal-tested 2d Marine Division's unexpectedly bloody assault at Tarawa, in the Central Pacific's Gilbert Islands in late November 1943, was followed in January and February by the 4th Marine Division's relatively easy victory at Kwajalein Atoll in the eastern Marshall Islands and the independent 22d Marine Regiment's three storm landings in Eniwetok Atoll in the western Marshalls.

Marine infantrymen overran the Japanese airfield on Guadalcanal, which precipitated a bitter six-month air, naval, and ground campaign of epic proportions. *National Archives and Records Administration*

Marine infantrymen and airmen, naive and undertrained at first but quickly battle hardened and better equipped, traveled a long and difficult road from Guadalcanal through the Marshalls. The island campaigns of 1942, 1943, and early 1944 forged four combat-tested divisions that provided veterans around whom two additional divisions were formed. Together, the six Marine divisions and four Marine aircraft wings blazed a legendary trail across the central and western Pacific, from Saipan to Tinian, to Guam, to Peleliu, to Iwo Jima, and then to Okinawa, the very doorstep to the Japanese home islands.

Islands of Hell is an intense pictorial record of the United States Marines in action in the western Pacific during the grinding last year of the Pacific War. It is offered as a respectful—a loving—tribute to all the young men who died there and then, and to the old warriors still living who strain to hear the last bugle call that will summon them to their turn at guarding Heaven's scenes.

Newly landed Marines take cover to search for Japanese defenders of Roi Island in Kwajalein Atoll. *Official USMC Photo*

GLOSSARY AND GUIDE TO ABBREVIATIONS

IIIAC III Amphibious Corps

VAC V Amphibious Corps

Amtrac Amphibian tractor

B-24 U.S. Army Air Forces Consolidated Liberator four-engine heavy bomber

B-25 U.S. Army Air Forces North American Mitchell twin-engine medium bomber

B-29 U.S. Army Air Forces Boeing Superfortress four-engine very-heavy bomber

BAR U.S. .30-caliber Browning automatic rifle

Bazooka U.S. 2.36-inch antitank/antiemplacement rocket launcher

Corsair U.S. Navy/Marine Vought F4U single-engine fighter

CVE Escort aircraft carrier

D-day Invasion day

D+1, etc. The day after D-day, etc.

DUKW U.S. wheeled amphibian truck

F4U U.S. Navy/Marine Vought Corsair single-engine fighter

F6F-5N U.S. Navy/Marine Grumman Hellcat night fighter

GI Government issue; slang for a U.S. Army soldier

HVAR High-velocity aerial rocket

J-day Tinian invasion day

L-day Okinawa invasion day

LCI(G) Landing craft, infantry (gunboat) armed with 20m and 40mm cannon

LCI(R) Landing craft, infantry (rocket) armed with rockets

LCVP Landing craft, vehicle, personnel

LSM Landing ship, medium

LVT Landing vehicle, tracked; amphibian tractor; amtrac

LVT(A) Armored amphibian tractor (i.e., amphibian tank)

MI U.S. Garand .30-caliber semi-automatic rifle

M3 U.S. .45-caliber submachine gun (aka "grease gun")

M3 U.S. Stuart light tank

M3 U.S. 75mm tank destroyer halftrack

M4 U.S. Sherman medium tank

M7 U.S. tracked tank destroyer with 105mm howitzer

MAG Marine Air Group

OY U.S. Marine light observation-spotter plane

PBJ U.S. Marine Corps designation for the North American B-25 Mitchell twin-engine medium bomber

Pioneers U.S. Marine shore party troops

Seabee Member of U.S. Navy construction battalions (CBs)

Sherman U.S. M4 medium tank

TBM U.S. Navy/Marine Grumman Avenger carrier torpedo/light bomber

TBS Talk better ships battalion- and regiment-level radio

VMF U.S. Marine fighter squadron

VMF(N) U.S. Marine night fighter squadron

VMO U.S. Marine observation squadron

W-day Guam invasion day

Josh. 11:20

Pacific Theater of Operations
May 1944

Kamchatka Pen.

Bering Sea

Attu Aleutian Islands

Kiska

Paramushir

CANADA

Vancouver

Seattle

Portland

UNITED STATES

San Francisco

Los Ang

PACIFIC OCEAN

Midway U.S.

Marcus Island Japan

Hawaiian Islands

Kauai Oahu Maui
U.S. Hawaii

Wake Island U.S.

Enewetak

Kwajalein

Marshall

Majuro

Panape

Palmyra

n e s Islands

d s Kusaie

Fanning

Christmas

s i Gilbert Islands Tarawa

Australian Mandate

Nauru British Mandate

Jarvis

a

Canton

Solomon

Choiseul Santa Isabel

Great Britain

Phoenix Islands

United States Great Britain

eorgia Islands Malaita

Ellice Islands

Marquesas Islands

Guadalcanal
San Cristobal

Santa Cruz Islands

U.S. N.Z.

Rennell

s i

N.Z. Mand.

Tokelau

Gt. Br. & Fr. Condominiam

Wallis

U.S.

Espiritu Santo
Malakula

a

Fr.

Samoa Islands

Tuamotu Archipelago

Étaté

New Hebridies

Vanua Levu

FRENCH France

France

Fiji Islands

Viti Levu

New Zealand

Society Islands Tahiti POLYNESIA

S e a

New Caladonia

Tonga Islands

Cook Islands

Japanese-held territories as of May 31, 1944

Pre-WWII mandates and possessions are shown in red type.

Part I

THE
MARIANAS

★ ★ ★ ★ ★

Official USMC Photo

INTRODUCTION

✯ ✯ ✯ ✯ ✯

THE AMERICAN MID-1944 CAMPAIGN in the Mariana Islands was an important strategic step in that it put Tokyo and the rest of Japan's industrial heartland within the range of the new U.S. Army Air Forces B-29 very-long-range bombers. Once the islands were secured and the airfields were built, the army air forces in the Pacific could do to Japanese industry what their counterparts in Europe had been doing to German industry since mid-1943. And then there was Guam, an American possession that had fallen to a Japanese invasion force at the very start of the war, its tiny Marine garrison sent into captivity. For Marines, retaking Guam would be payback and the fulfillment of a blood oath.

Even though these important objectives had been accorded an early place in prewar strategic planning, the shape of the Pacific War had left them alone for two and a half years of hard battles in the Solomon Islands and at the far eastern periphery of Japanese central Pacific holding: first Tarawa in November 1943, then the Marshall Islands in January and February 1944. Then air bases had to be improved and developed in the western Marshalls so that American land-based bombers could reconnoiter and soften Saipan, Tinian, Guam, and other Japanese bases in the Marianas. It was a tried-and-true procedure, but painstaking.

These Marines are getting ready to rush a Japanese position. *Official USMC Photo*

Official USMC Photo

1
SAIPAN

★ ★ ★ ★ ★

June 15–July 9, 1944

THE STRATEGIC SITUATION

SO FAR, THE CENTRAL PACIFIC DRIVE had been a complete vindication of American strategic pronouncements and planning going back to 1913. Back then, the scheme to seize and hold a line of bases that unfolded from east to west—from Hawaii to Japan—had been in service of maintaining the strategic weapon of the day, the mighty surface fleet built around a solid core of battleships. By 1943, the solid core of the strategic advance across the wide Pacific had become a burgeoning carrier fleet supplemented by land-based bombers escorted by land-based fighters. Nevertheless, the execution of the American drive was a nearly picture-perfect implementation of the early vision.

It had been a painstaking advance in 1942, 1943, and early 1944, but now the tempo was to hit overdrive, for a new paradigm was about to emerge. If a string of advancing fleet bases looked old-fashioned and clunky in just 1942, a string of advancing bases tied to the range of land-based fighters looked even more clunky by early 1944. This was because the U.S. Army Air Forces had in its hands the means to strike the Japanese heartland itself from as far away as the Mariana Islands. And the Marianas happened to be the next logical target of the two-year-old strategy based on the need to mount new assaults on islands that could first be bombarded and reconnoitered at some length by multiengine land-based bombers that could be escorted by land-based fighters.

So if the island-hopping basing strategy that had dragged the Allies forward from Samoa to Wallis Island to the Ellice Islands to the Gilbert Islands to the Marshall Islands had made *tactical* sense in the age of land-based fighters and long-range bombers, the hop from the Marshall Islands to the Mariana Islands made sense in the *strategic* possibilities that could be available in the emerging age of land-based *very*-long-range bombers, B-29s. By luck more than desire, the Marianas were not only close enough to Japan for the B-29s to reach the Japanese industrial heartland, but also the islands themselves were large enough to support

The Japanese had acquired the Mariana Islands after World War I. They had more than twenty years in which to fortify them. They did a decent job of it when they were pushed into it as the war—of their choosing—went increasingly against them. The 5.5-inch dual-purpose naval gun shown in the first photo is beautifully sited, and the craftsmanship that went into the position's construction is admirable. But it is very difficult to comprehend how the same defenders who paid so much attention to detail when they built this position could have neglected entirely the emplacement—in any sort of position—of the at least nine 5.5-inch guns shown in the second photo, which are only a few such unmounted weapons the American invaders discovered on Saipan. *Official USMC Photos*

the massive bases the B-29s required to mount a meaningfully large and efficient bombardment campaign against that Japanese industrial heartland.

When detailed planning for the Marianas campaign began, the B-29 was still untested in war. There were no bases in the Pacific that could accommodate the giant bombers, and no targets in the Pacific save Japan itself that were worth the effort of building bases for these airplanes. Instead, from early 1944, B-29s were flown to India and China in the hope of striking Japan from that direction, but the B-29 would be able to reach Japan from the Marianas when large islands there could be seized and adequate facilities could be built. Thus, for the time being, the Pacific island-hopping strategy was co-opted by an even higher-level strategic requirement for B-29 bases from which the centers of Japanese industrial power, 1,200 miles away, could be reached. Luckily, the program for standing up new B-29 units and the progress of the Pacific War dovetailed perfectly in mid-1944. If the requisite bases fell into American hands, there would be B-29 groups ready to use them by the time runways and infrastructure were in place.

✫ ✫ ✫

A direct hit by a large-caliber naval shell ripped open this steel-reinforced bunker and disabled the large-caliber gun within. *Official USMC Photo*

JN. 14:6

Marines clamber down cargo nets from their transport to an LCVP for a ride all or part of the way into one of Saipan's D-day invasion beaches. *Official USMC Photo*

An army LVT(A) crosses a coral reef on its way to the beach. This early version of the armored amtrac is equipped with a 37mm gun in its gun mount as well as a pair of machine guns in a compartment behind the mount. LVT(A)-4s, also used at Saipan, were each armed with a 75mm short-barrel howitzer and one .50-caliber machine gun in an open mount. The 75mm howitzer could be used to supplement artillery. None of the armored amtracs was particularly well armored because of weight restrictions, so they were used only sparingly, if at all, in combat much beyond the beachhead. *Official USMC Photo*

ORGANIZATION

The organization and arms available to Marine divisions had been in flux since the start of the war. Two factors were in play: needs based on lessons learned that could be projected into the next campaign, and the growing strength of the American industrial base.

In the first case, an ongoing problem that had yet to be licked was shore party support at the beachhead. It was known that the violence of island warfare could not tolerate even the temporary use of combat troops in a supply-handling role, so the Marine Corps beefed up

At a point 1,500 yards from shore, a 4th Marine Division rifle squad cross-decks from an LCVP to an army LVT-3, a new type of amtrac equipped with a rear ramp by which the troops could exit while using the bulk of the amtrac as cover from enemy fire. There were not enough Marine amtracs to support the landing of two Marine divisions at Saipan, so the army unit was used to fill out the V Amphibious Corps' needs. *Official USMC Photo*

First-wave amtracs in the company of LVT(A) amphibian tanks charge toward the beach at top speed, about 4 knots. *Official USMC Photo*

its pioneer (shore party) units and drew on U.S. Navy Seabee (naval construction) battalions attached to the Marine divisions for beach work, then stood up depot and ammunition units for overseeing dumps. Too many amphibian tractors (amtracs) were needed for a divisional assault for the divisional organization to handle, so independent amtrac battalions were stood up as corps troops and, in the wake of the Marshalls operation, the organic divisional amtrac units were reassigned as corps troops. Although trained to build roads and the like, Marine engineer battalions had been used in the assault role—demolitions and flamethrowers—since Tarawa, and this role was beefed up by training and the availability of many more flamethrower and demolitions teams, so the task of building and maintaining roads fell more heavily on

As the army amtrac behind it burns, crewmen (wearing life vests) and passengers from the near army amtrac risk their lives to drop off a load of ammunition and other supplies on one of the 4th Marine Division beaches.
Official USMC Photo

As occurred on many D-day mornings across the Pacific, many combat troops who were not able or not inspired to attack from a stalled assault landing became passive as the frustrations mounted. No one is leading these Marines into battle, and they are not ready to lead themselves. *Official USMC Photo*

This trio has attempted to move ahead, but Japanese fire is too intense and, worst of all, the sources of the fire are probably invisible. *Official USMC Photo*

Meanwhile, problems mount. Because of overcrowding behind whatever cover and concealment the inland verges of the beach offer, it becomes difficult to land more troops, much ammunition, or other supplies. This leads to congestion at the surf line, and that throws off the schedules the amtrac crews have been called on to meet. So in addition to damaged amtracs taken out of service while the beaches were uncongested, amtracs caught in traffic jams with sorely needed follow-on troops and supplies are not only slowed, they also are made more vulnerable to defensive fires for longer than is worth the risk of whatever their crews think they can accomplish. *Official USMC Photo*

Seabees attached to the divisions as well as on an independent Marine engineer battalion organized for use at the corps level.

In 1944, a cornucopia of weapons allowed Marine infantry units at all levels to be upgraded and reorganized. All the infantry squads were reorganized into thirteen-man units consisting of a squad leader and three four-man fire teams, and each fire team was built around a Browning Automatic Rifle (BAR). Divisional special weapons (antitank) battalions were disbanded and regimental heavy weapons companies received additional 37mm antitank guns and M3 tank destroyers (halftracks mounting 75mm antitank/antibunker guns).

The availability of more 105mm howitzers caused the conversion of one 75mm battalion per divisional artillery regiment to a second 105mm battalion, and several independent 105mm and 155mm battalions were added as corps troops. Armored

And then—as has always happened in Marine Corps history—a sparkplug ignites the stalled engine of war. Here, a troop leader—a sergeant or a lieutenant, or perhaps a private with command presence—decides that his honor is at stake, or that it's dumber to be a sitting, passive target than a moving, aggressive warrior. So he stands up and hurls an order or a challenge to all who can hear: "Follow me!" And because many of those other men feel their own honor or manhood has been compromised, the mindset they have been brutally drilled to attain kicks back in, and suddenly a gaggle of timid individuals is transformed into a fully integrated machine made for taking war to the enemy. *Official USMC Photo*

The wrecked and the wounded. And the honored dead, who fell with their faces to the foe. *Official USMC Photos*

A Marine LVT(A) armed with a 75mm howitzer (at right) and three army LVT(A)s armed with 37mm guns form a skirmish line on the smoky D-day battlefield as Marine infantry form up for an advance. *Official USMC Photo*

The advance turns wary as the Marines move into dense brush. There's something out ahead these Marines can smell, and they don't like it. *Official USMC Photo*

amphibian battalions also were added as corps troops, and new LVT(A)-4 armored amtracs, each wielding a short-barrel 75mm howitzer and a .50-caliber machine gun, replaced most of the older 37mm-armed LVT(A)s.

In sum, each Marine division was about two thousand men smaller than it had been, but each was significantly more lethal. This was a bit of excellent timing, because Saipan, the first objective in the Marianas, was seen as a significantly tougher proposition than any previous objective. At 72 square miles, it was much larger than any objective in the Gilberts and the Marshalls, yet significantly smaller in land area than any objective in the Solomons. The problem was that every inch of Saipan was or could be defended in considerable strength by an estimated thirty-one thousand troops, so a weeks-long battle of the intensity of Tarawa was foreseen.

✵ ✵ ✵

continued on page 16

A rudimentary Japanese pillbox, large enough for several defenders and a machine gun. *Official USMC Photo*

These Marines are getting ready to rush a Japanese position. *Official USMC Photo*

A .30-caliber light machine gun is deployed to cover advancing riflemen or to suppress fire from a Japanese position the riflemen are positioning themselves to attack. The extremely portable light machine guns were organized with 60mm mortars and, as the war progressed, .30-caliber medium machine guns into an infantry company's weapons platoon. *Official USMC Photo*

The flamethrower was the infantry weapon of choice when dealing with a well-defended or well-camouflaged Japanese position. By mid-1944, there were numerous flamethrowers assigned down to the company level, and they were used as much as possible. But they suffered from limited effective range, so they had to be used under conditions that favored them, usually when targets could be suppressed by heavy gunfire. The best approach by the flamethrower assaultman was from a blind corner, but then he might inadvertently expose himself to fire from other defensive positions undiscovered to that point. Getting a flamethrower close enough to an objective to do its job always started with a leap of faith or a position of complete fatalism. *Official USMC Photo*

A bazooka team makes its way to the front from Beach Green. The 2.36-inch (60mm) bazooka rocket can take out some defensive positions, but not all. It's worth a try. *Official USMC Photo*

The 37mm antitank gun had been completely outclassed in Europe by increasingly bigger and tougher German tanks, but it remained a useful weapon in the Pacific against fairly crude and underarmored Japanese tanks. It was employed most and best against pillboxes and bunkers. Often the 37mm armor-piercing round could penetrate a log wall, or a high-explosive or even a canister round could be fired through an embrasure. In a pinch against a concrete bunker, the extremely accurate antitank gun could fire over and over at roughly the same spot until it finally broke through. The holes in the shield of the antitank gun seen here are simple bullet holes, which could be worrying. *Official USMC Photo*

There's always another Japanese position beyond the one you just overcame. *Official USMC Photo*

Continued from page 13
THE PLAN

Saipan was slated for assault on June 15, 1944, by the veteran 2d and 4th Marine divisions, with the U.S. Army's veteran 27th Infantry Division in reserve. Once a beachhead was established, it was felt that at least two and probably all three divisions would undertake a continuous assault to clear the island, then go on to land on adjacent Tinian and do the same. As soon as possible after the landing on Saipan, at least one of the existing airfields would be rehabilitated and improved to provide land-based air support for the ongoing fighting and the invasion of Tinian. Thereafter, the island's air bases would be improved for B-29s and to support the neutralization from the air of bypassed Japanese bases in the Marianas. Until local air support got up and running, the ground campaign would be supported by carrier air, naval gunfire, and divisional and corps artillery.

The Saipan and Tinian operations would be overseen in their entirety by V Amphibious Corps (VAC), a Marine-run organization. The Guam operation would be overseen by III Amphibious Corps (IIIAC, formerly designated I Marine Amphibious Corps, or IMAC), also a Marine-run organization.

✿ ✿ ✿

continued on page 20

New radio packs have been distributed to company commanders for keeping in touch with platoon leaders, the battalion command post, and artillery forward observers, who all have access to good portable radios for the first time in the Pacific War. Previously, runners had to be sent on lonely message runs from which they didn't always return. *Official USMC Photo*

Wire communications were still in heavy use. Miles and miles of communications wire set on the ground were vulnerable to enemy and friendly fire as well as vehicle tracks and wheels. Constant maintenance by wire repair teams was required. Nevertheless, wire communications was necessary because the radios of the day had limited battery power and range, and they could be maddeningly balky. *Official USMC Photo*

This is the first artillery forward observer team to get into action on Saipan; it is directing fire for 75mm pack howitzers of the 2d Marine Division's 10th Marines. In addition to the two forward observers (one is usually enough) is a bodyguard (with M1 rifle) and a communicator, who is holding the handset of a wire-dependent sound-powered telephone that links him to a battalion or battery fire direction center. The team locates targets from a front-line post, relays coordinates to the fire direction center, orders the fire mission (how many and what type of artillery rounds), and adjusts the fire as needed. Mortars are directed in pretty much the same manner. This observation post appears to be manned by two forward observers. *Official USMC Photo*

A 75mm pack howitzer in action. The small size of this weapon, coupled with its ability to be broken down and carried by its gun crew, made it ideal for amphibious operations, because it could go ashore early in light landing craft or even amtracs. As the war progressed, an artillery regiment went from fielding three 75mm pack howitzer battalions to fielding just one. The 75s were replaced with 105mm howitzers, which were less portable but a lot more lethal and destructive. *Official USMC Photo*

A 105mm howitzer is wheeled into a firing position by its crew. The 105 was a splendid weapon, a modern homegrown system the army first acquired in very small numbers in the late 1930s, before they were placed in mass production and replaced older, smaller weapons in the standard infantry division "light" artillery battalion. By August 1942, the Marine Corps put its first 105mm battalion into combat, at Guadalcanal. The Marine 105s were considered "medium" artillery throughout World War II because the 75mm pack howitzers remained in the divisional artillery regiments as "light" artillery.
Official USMC Photo

Marine 155mm "heavy" artillery ("medium" to the army, which eventually fielded 8-inch artillery) came in two flavors, howitzers and guns. The 155 seen here is a howitzer from the 2d Separate 155mm Howitzer Battalion, a unit assigned directly to the V Amphibious Corps for use at its discretion. *Official USMC Photo*

The 81mm mortar was the Marine infantry battalion commander's personal artillery. Shown here, in the first photo, the gunner is laying the mortar for a fire mission while a communicator takes details via a sound-powered telephone. The assistant gunner is to the right of the mortar and two ammunition carriers are also shown, as is a supply of ready ammunition. In the second photo, the round has just left the tube. *Official USMC Photos*

Continued from page 16
INVASION

Beginning at 0812 hours on June 15, 1944, the lead waves of the 2d and 4th Marine divisions began the final lap of their assault on Saipan's southwestern shore. Each division was led by two reinforced regiments (now known as regimental combat teams), which in turn were each led by two reinforced infantry battalions (now known as battalion landing teams). From north to south, the regiments were arrayed as follows: the 6th Marine Regiment (6th Marines), then the 8th Marines, covered the 2d Marine Division front of 2,400 yards ending at Afetna Point; then the 4th Marine Division's 23d Marines landing south of Afetna Point directly against the sizable town of Charan Kanoa; then the 25th Marines landing on the southernmost beaches from south of Charan Kanoa to Agingan Point. The objective of all four combat teams was to advance a mile or more inland to the day's phase line, then resume the assault all the way across the southern third of Saipan, including Aslito Airdrome. The 2d Marines; the 24th Marines; and the independent 1st Battalion, 29th Marines (1/29), made

Each Marine infantry company fielded a section of three extremely portable 60mm mortars as part of its weapons platoon. Quite often, the 60mm squads were close enough to the front lines to see their target and adjust their own fire, but the mortar section was organized to respond to calls and adjustments from front-line observers, sometimes by radio or field telephone, but often simply shouted. The ammunition types were smoke or high explosive. *Official USMC Photo*

The .30-caliber medium machine gun was rarely used in the assault or in a battle of movement; it was too cumbersome. But given enough time to reach the front lines, it could be used to cover advancing Marines with overhead or long-range suppressive fire, and in a war of movement it was deployed on the front lines every day at the close of action to bolster and anchor the night defenses. Early in the war the medium machine guns were organized into machine gun platoons in an infantry battalion weapons company. By mid-1944, many divisions had stood down the weapons companies and pushed the medium machine guns down to the infantry companies' enlarged weapons platoons. *Official USMC Photo*

As Marine infantry moves forward, these Marine engineers comb a beach area for mines and booby traps. This was not an invasion beach, but it is probably needed for getting supplies ashore. *Official USMC Photo*

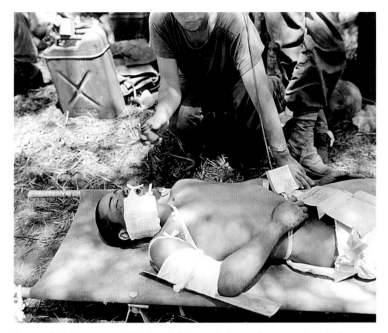

A wounded Japanese soldier is administered plasma by a navy hospital corpsman after he has been picked up on the battlefield. If he makes it as far as a front-line aid station, a wounded Japanese will be treated as well as a wounded American. *Official USMC Photo*

A dead Marine is covered with a poncho, and his upright rifle marks the spot for graves registration teams that comb the battlefield to recover fallen Marines. The dead Japanese soldier in the trench will also be buried by Marines. *Official USMC Photo*

a feint toward several beaches in northwestern Saipan. They kept Japanese reinforcements from rushing south, but they didn't draw any of the southern forces northward.

The landing, beginning at 0843, was marred by ineffective final bombardments and air attacks. There was too much ground for the naval and aerial bombardment to cover. Moreover, the 6th and 8th Marines drifted between 400 and 600 yards north of their assigned beaches due to an unanticipated heavy northward current. Defenses at the beach were far heavier and better camouflaged than anticipated, and they were overcome only through sheer determination and a great deal of blood.

The plan of the 6th and 8th Marines was to alight from their amtracs and follow-on landing craft, reorganize, and advance inland on foot. The leading elements of the 23d and 25th Marines planned to advance while remaining aboard their amtracs. All the regiments counted heavily on support from LVT(A)s.

The 6th Marines, on Beach Red, fought inland about one hundred yards in the face of plunging fire from machine guns,

Many Japanese soldiers were killed and a number of their tanks were disabled or destroyed in a series of uncoordinated attacks during the night of June 15. *Official USMC Photo*

The Marines drove ahead far and wide on June 16 and 17. The Japanese resisted and delayed where they could, sometimes quite effectively, but Marines and the 27th Infantry Division broke out of the confined beachhead area to their key early objectives by maintaining pressure at all points. *Official USMC Photos*

mortars, and artillery emplaced on the ridgeline that was the regimental objective. Several small tank attacks had to be beaten back as well. By 1300 hours, the regiment had suffered losses as high as 35 percent, including the commander of 2/6 and his executive officer. By the end of the day, every available rifleman was on the line, which was 400 yards inland at its deepest point.

Just to the south, on Beach Green, the 8th Marines' two assault battalions had been driven together by the current, and both had landed in the northern half of the regimental zone, albeit with few casualties. The assault battalions quickly sorted themselves out, and 3/8 attacked inland, as planned. Company G, 2/8, attacked southward toward Afetna Point, using the coastal road as a boundary. By nightfall, the northern half of Afetna Point was in Marine hands and seven of nine antiboat guns in beachside positions had been silenced. The rest of 2/8 advanced toward Lake Susupe but became isolated in marshland and had to withdraw before nightfall. Two reserve battalions—1/8 and 1/29—also landed on Beach Green during the day. Both were broken up to seal various gaps. By the end of D-day, the reinforced 8th Marines was isolated from the regiments on either flank and, stymied

Here lies a Marine machine gunner, temporarily interred on the spot on which he died after he sustained a direct hit by a Japanese mortar round. His grave is marked by his shattered carbine. *Official USMC Photo*

These haggard Marines are taking a needed and deserved break from the fighting under cover of a Japanese artillery piece. *Official USMC Photo*

by the marshes, had not fully secured its day's objectives. The commanders of 2/8 and 3/8 were wounded in the day's fighting.

The 23d Marines, landing on Beach Green from Afetna Point across Charan Kanoa, faced little opposition at the beach. Still mounted in its LVTs, it reorganized and advanced inland. Troops from 3/23 mounted in eight LVTs and supported by three LVT(A)-4s charged straight down the road through Charan Kanoa, all the way to the regimental objective atop Mount Fina Sisu. They were subjected to heavy fire through the day and had to withdraw during the night because no other friendly units could get so far forward. Similarly, troops in three LVTs accompanied by five LVT(A)s fought through to the 2/23 phase line, but they also were withdrawn in the dark. The same marshes that had stymied 2/8 to the north also stymied the 23d Marines, which came up well short of its D-day goals despite opposition so light that the regimental reserve battalion, 1/23, wasn't even committed.

The 25th Marines, mounted in army LVTs, landed on Beach Yellow in the standard two-battalion assault. On the left, 2/25, which was supported by army LVT(A)-4s, overcame small-arms fire and advanced through heavy artillery and mortar fire to a rail line that ran diagonally across its front between 500 and 700 yards inland. To the right, the VAC right-flank battalion, 1/25, was stopped cold just inland from the beach, and many LVTs were forced to retract under intense fire before supplies and gear could be unloaded. The bulk of the defensive fire was based on Agingan Point, beyond 1/25's right flank. The Japanese constantly attacked northward from the point, but by early afternoon, once 3/25 and a company of 4th Tank Battalion Sherman M4 medium tanks had been committed to support 1/25, the Marines sealed the flank once and for all. Indeed, the 25th Marines was able to conduct a steady advance inland despite the contest on its right flank, and by day's end the entire regiment had advanced to its phase line between 700 and 2,000 yards inland.

Throughout the beachhead, once naval gunfire observers were ashore, the naval bombardment was highly accurate, as was aerial bombardment guided by observers in the front lines. The pinpoint accuracy of the supporting arms was something of a marvel. And the advances, such as they were, owed much success to tanks and LVT(A)-4s, even though many tanks and armored amtracs went astray, were lost in accidents, or were knocked out by enemy fire from the heights. Seven of nine divisional artillery battalions also

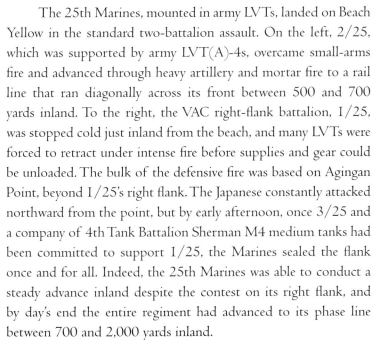

As the battle opened out into broader reaches, amtracs took on most of the burden for moving chores all across the VAC arena. *Official USMC Photos*

The first built-up area the VAC offensive reached was the sugar-refining center at Charan Kanoa. Here, the veteran island fighters of the 2d and 4th Marine divisions came upon the first urban combat Marines faced in the Pacific. They had had no training for street fighting, so they made it up on the run, using their veterans' instincts to make a go of it. *Official USMC Photos*

were landed on D-day, but many of the 14th Marines' howitzers were mislanded, and Japanese mortars knocked out four 4/14 105mm howitzers.

It was later estimated that D-day casualties totaled two thousand killed and wounded, more or less, but by nightfall the troops had advanced inland from four hundred yards in the north to two thousand yards in the south. Plenty of supplies were ashore, the medical evacuation system was working, and all but two reserve infantry battalions were ashore to plug gaps or await breakthroughs they could exploit. In sum, the beachhead had been well established, albeit at great cost.

The Japanese mounted numerous counterattacks during the night, most heavily against the 6th Marines, where tanks were used. All these attacks were beaten back, some quite easily. As far as the troops were concerned, they would face hundreds fewer dug-in Japanese the next day.

ABANDONED

During D-day, the high command learned that a vast Imperial navy carrier and surface armada had been put in motion toward Saipan. There was no great surprise in this; all thinking about a war with Japan had always contemplated a decisive naval battle as its culmination. That the Japanese were making their move at Saipan was no great shock either, as both sides considered the Marianas to be the outer line of the empire itself. The Japanese carriers had not been seen since October 1942, and their battleships had not been seen since November 1942. If they

Elements of the 4th Marine Division captured the approaches to Aslito Airdrome, but the facility fell to 27th Infantry Division units that were used to replace elements of both Marine divisions in clearing the remainder of southern Saipan. *Official USMC Photo*

Marine riflemen leapfrog forward under fire in northern Saipan. *Official USMC Photo*

This pair of Marine engineer assaultmen flee as a TNT charge they have just set blows up an underground bunker. *Official USMC Photo*

were going to be of some use in the Pacific, Saipan almost had to be the place, and mid-June 1944 had to be the time.

The American admirals reacted by postponing the June 18 Guam invasion indefinitely and ordering all transports and landing ships to sail east, out of range, by the night of June 17–18. Inasmuch as the beachhead was fairly deep by the end of D-day, as many supplies as possible were to be landed in good order as quickly as possible. The VAC commanding general also decided to land two-thirds of the 27th Infantry Division that was his Saipan reserve; the D-day fighting had been heavy enough to warrant the landing of at least a regiment, and nobody knew when the transports might return. No doubt, the GIs would come in handy. Attacks by carrier aircraft were expected, so army and Marine antiaircraft units also were rushed ashore. The last of all these reinforcements landed after dark on July 17, and the transport fleet sailed east—for a week. By then, Navy amphibian patrol bombers were operating from a seaplane anchorage off the invasion beaches.

THE SOUTHERN DRIVE

The fighting on June 16 and 17 was heavy, and it proved to be decisive. The 4th Marine Division and attached army units fought to the edge of Aslito Airdrome, Marines fully secured Charan Kanoa and Afetna Point, and the 2d Marine Division fought inland into the high ground overlooking the northern beachhead. The only delays were in the marshlands around Lake Susupe, but

even this vexing terrain was overcome at the divisional boundary on June 17. Moreover, the Japanese mounted a large tank-supported night attack that did little lasting damage and mainly thinned their own ranks. Also, a counterlanding mounted on the night of June 17–18 from the northwestern coast was turned back with heavy losses when engaged by artillery and surface warships. Night attacks by Japanese torpedo bombers based at Truk,

A 37mm antitank gun, its crew perfectly arrayed, snipes back at a covey of Japanese snipers holding a front-line defensive position. *Official USMC Photo*

Even though this Marine is getting timely front-line care for a wound that does not look serious, he will be dead in a few hours. *Official USMC Photo*

Hand grenades and Molotov cocktails were used as stand-off weapons when the Marines and Japanese were fighting at close quarters from defilade positions and as means to at least partially sanitize a cave if something more compelling, such as demolitions charges or a flamethrower, was not readily at hand. *Official USMC Photos*

in the Caroline Islands, were largely beaten back, but an LCT was fatally damaged, an LST was damaged, and an escort aircraft carrier was severely damaged. Basically, these land, amphibious, and air attacks failed to make a dent. With or without its fleet of transports and cargo ships—and even in the face of a massive naval confrontation—VAC was so firmly embedded on Saipan with so many supplies at its disposal that the fate of the invasion was not the least bit in doubt.

Marine riflemen advance through a farmstead behind an artillery barrage that has laid waste to buildings and crops. *Official USMC Photo*

This bazookaman is about to undertake a live-fire test to gauge the effects of a 2.36-inch antitank rocket against a cave whose mouth is protected by a sandbag wall.
Official USMC Photo

Given the firepower at his beck and call, it might seem surprising that this Marine is approaching the entrance of a cave with only a .45-caliber pistol in hand. He must have good reason to believe he is on an errand of mercy.
Official USMC Photo

These Marines have dropped a smoke grenade into the entrance of an underground cave and now wait to see if the smoke drifts up from other holes in the ground. This will indicate the size and complexity of a potentially large underground bunker system. *Official USMC Photo*

During the rush to clear decks for the upcoming naval battle, Marines flying OY observation planes came ashore from escort carriers to locate paths to and around Japanese positions and to spot artillery fire and air attacks. The OYs, based initially on Beach Yellow and Charan Kanoa, were operated by VMO-2 and VMO-4 and were often flown by volunteer enlisted pilots. (The innovation had originated with an ad hoc 1st Marine Division squadron using borrowed army spotter planes at Cape Gloucester.)

THE NORTHERN DRIVE

Elements of the 4th Marine Division drove to the southeastern coast on June 18, which cut off the Japanese in southeastern Saipan from the rest of the defense force. The 4th Division next

The Marianas had been heavily settled by Japanese colonists in the years after World War I, and there were thousands of Korean laborers and native Chamorro tribespeople on Saipan as well. They went into hiding as soon as the invasion threat became plain, and Marines were on their guard to spare them whenever humanly possible. Unfortunately, many Japanese and Korean civilians were held hostage by Japanese troops whose command system had broken down. They were used as slave labor to build and improve defenses as well as hostages for purposes no one can adequately explain beyond an exaggeration of Bushido principles by low-ranking soldiers. *Official USMC Photo*

pivoted northeast of Lake Susupe to join the 2d Division on June 21 along a steep, hilly line stretching across Saipan on the southern side of Mount Tapotchau to Magicienne Bay. The unoccupied areas of southeastern Saipan were left to the 27th Infantry Division.

It was no romp. Many of the Japanese units were first-rate—well trained and highly skilled soldiers and naval infantry who sold their lives at great cost. Others were cannon fodder who died in badly conceived counterattacks that accomplished nothing of value to their cause. The terrain was a horrible mix of lowland cane fields on table-flat land dominated by hills or mountains, or the steep-sided, ravine-cut hills and mountains themselves, where Japanese troops lay in wait in invisible dominating positions that had to be torn down toe-to-toe by infantrymen. Moreover, bad planning had denied the Marine

Medium tanks and halftracks line up to deliver direct fire on a nearby objective in the 4th Marine Division zone of action.
Official USMC Photo

This M3 antitank halftrack has stood off to duel at least one Japanese tank making a stand farther up this road. Smoke rises from the distant tank, and many 75mm shell casings litter the roadway beside the halftrack.
Official USMC Photo

This 4th Tank Battalion medium tank's 75mm main gun is set to deliver high-angle artillery fire on a distant objective. While the 75mm short-barrel howitzers aboard LVT(A)s were often used as artillery, the 75mm guns aboard tanks were rarely used for this purpose, even though they were equipped to handle artillery missions. *Official USMC Photo*

divisions replacements, and the fleet's week-long departure added to that miscalculation; Marine unit strength and fighting power had trended downward to the tune of 6,165 dead, wounded, or missing from the first shot onward.

The fleet and light carrier air groups of Task Force 58 tore the heart out of Japanese carrier aviation on June 19 and 20 in the utterly one-sided Battle of the Philippine Sea, the Marianas Turkey Shoot. It was, as many prewar planners had foreseen, the grand fleet action that doomed one side to certain defeat. Even if Japan no longer had a real hope of winning the Pacific War, the Japanese thought they would never be ready to stop the killing and dying.

Eight Army Air Forces fighter-bombers operating from Aslito Airdrome supported Marine ground units in the inauguration of VAC's all-out northern attack on June 22. The Marines unknowingly hit the Japanese main line of resistance that day. Determined defenders numbering nearly ten thousand well-led and well-equipped Imperial Army troops and five

continued on page 42

A Marine rifle squad probes warily ahead at the tip of the advance farther into northern Saipan. All the heavy weapons in the world cannot advance over rough terrain the way infantrymen can, and none other has the sensitivity to hear and smell and literally feel the presence of hidden enemy soldiers. *Official USMC Photo*

Sometimes the best-honed battlefield sensitivity cannot alter the fate of individuals. *Official USMC Photo*

This Japanese light machine gunner was shot to death as he hurriedly set up against Marines who had been dogging his heels through wooded terrain. *Official USMC Photo*

The fall of Mount Tapotchau and other heights in central Saipan gave Marine observers unparalleled vistas over most of northern Saipan and provided amplified command and control possibilities. *Official USMC Photo*

Garapan

The 2d Marines, which landed farthest north on D-day, pivoted to the north to protect the beaches as most of the rest of VAC units extended across the island or southward. When the main bodies of the two Marine divisions turned their attention to the northern half of Saipan, the 2d Marines remained as the anchor regiment on the western coast, which brought it face-to-face with Saipan's largest settlement, Garapan, a small city in the true sense of the word. Until Saipan, Marines had never tackled urban combat. So they learned how as they waded into Garapan's mean streets.

The reorganization of Marine infantry squads into four-man fire teams came just in time for the urban warfare on Saipan. It took no effort whatsoever for the tactics of clearing buildings to break up the integrity of so large a unit as a rifle squad. Fortunately, the selection and training of fire-team leaders assured good tactical control at the level of only three or four men needed to check out a small house beyond the sight of more senior troop leaders. *Official USMC Photo*

The first steps to clearing Garapan were devoted to tightening a noose around the built-up area, to seal the town off from supplies and reinforcements. This was accomplished over largely open terrain by the 2d and 6th Marines in days leading up to the assault into the built-up area. *Official USMC Photo*

It didn't take much to run a Marine infantry company in 1944—a few good officers and plenty of communications gear. Here, a company commander is on the company's portable battery-powered radio, probably with the battalion command post; the Marine at the far left might be an artillery forward observer speaking with a battery fire direction center via sound-powered telephone; and the Marine at the far right is speaking on a walkie-talkie, probably with a rifle platoon commander. City fighting tended to balkanize infantry formations, but good communications balanced out the command-and-control problems imposed by limited vistas and challenges to unit cohesion. *Official USMC Photo*

A platoon commander or his radioman could receive orders and make requests while far from the eyes of senior officers. The device was a godsend in the shattered neighborhoods of Garapan. *Official USMC Photo*

Masonry and concrete were amply used in the construction of Garapan's buildings, walls, curbs, and wells. They and all manner of man-made objects were used to advantage by defenders and attackers alike—as hiding places, as obstructions that could be manipulated to channelize infantry into ambushes, as secondary shrapnel that could be used to deadly advantage by the detonation of explosive devices. *Official USMC Photos*

Razing buildings by artillery fire or direct demolition was one way to clear longer vistas, but longer vistas work to the advantage of both sides. Simply crossing a street can be deadly in urban combat, because savvy defenders will stake out such long, narrow open areas in full knowledge that the enemy has to cross sooner or later.
Official USMC Photo

Continued from page 36

thousand less-well-equipped naval infantrymen and sundry Imperial Army stragglers held the Americans to half the day's objectives. That night was the first in which there were no significant counterattacks, which indicated that the Japanese commanders had given up on defeating the invaders and were content to fight a battle of attrition.

The worst ground fighting lay ahead as the gallant and determined Marines attacked into determined and gallant Japanese holding high ground in extremely broken terrain. The names that Marines and the GIs who joined them there gave to terrain features say it all: Death Valley, Purple Heart Ridge, and Hell's Pocket.

An aerial view of Saipan's northern highlands, which provided formidable fighting terrain for both Marine divisions along the coasts and the 27th Infantry Division in the center. *Official USMC Photo*

Tanks and infantrymen working together was the norm when the ground suited it. Both partners had been trained to use their particular advantages and best attributes to help boost the fighting qualities of the other. Note in the first two photos that infantrymen are kneeling behind the tank's turret, so they can advise the tank commander about things they and their footborne comrades can see that the tank crew cannot see. If the riflemen are fired on, they will bunch up behind the tank until they can locate the source of the fire and, with aid of the tank crew, figure out how to overcome it. Meanwhile, and throughout a joint operation, the infantrymen will keep enemy soldiers armed with antitank weapons at a distance. In the last photo, a squad leader communicates with a tank commander via a field telephone rigged to the tank's left rear bumper. Undoubtedly, the two are trying to figure out how to overcome a defensive position at the lowest possible cost in American blood. Note the extra panel of "armor" that has been affixed to the tank's hull. It is a simple wooden board used to deter Japanese magnetic antitank mines.
Official USMC Photos

This Marine sniper is armed with a .30-caliber Springfield M1903 rifle equipped with a telescopic sight. *Official USMC Photo*

A Marine light flame tank burns off the scrub and probably incinerates a Japanese defensive position at the edge of a field. Flame tanks and flamethrowers could be used in the Pacific because the Japanese had refused to sign the Geneva conventions that prohibited their use against other signatories. Germany had signed the conventions, so American flame weapons were not used against its troops. *Official USMC Photo*

The 27th Infantry Division went into the line between the two Marine divisions on June 23, and right away there were complaints and retorts that the army was going too slow or the Marines were going too fast. The Marine VAC commander relieved the army division commander on June 25 and sparked a controversy that neither service has laid to rest since.

Americans prevailed in the atrocious battles for the northern half of Saipan, but it took thousands of tons of bombs and naval and artillery shells to help them do so. The ground battle was unremitting and exhausting, but the Americans kept going. In the end, the surviving Japanese troops were pushed back into the Marpi Point area, and here Americans saw the

This 2d Marine Division rifle platoon waits warily in combat formation while an advance element "sniffs" the road ahead.
Official USMC Photo

Locked and loaded and ready to go.
Official USMC Photo

By July 6, the Japanese defenders were in extremis. There was no hope of their holding the VAC offensive. At that point, the Japanese island commander ordered an all-out suicide attack by all the troops still under his actual control. Then he committed suicide. The "last banzai" began at 0400 hours, July 7. Its power and fury engulfed many VAC units. Two army battalions were overrun, and two Marine artillery batteries fought the enemy at arm's length with direct fire, then small-arms fire when their howitzers were overrun. Though hurt and dazed, the army and Marine units bearing the brunt of the attack either held their ground or contained the offensive after giving ground. *Official USMC Photos*

true face of the enemy. A mad, useless final "banzai" attack broke the Japanese defensive organization, but Japanese troops continued to hold out unto death in caves that honeycombed Mount Marpi. It would have been one thing if only Japanese troops held out here, but Saipan had been the center of a large, civilian-run sugar-growing and -processing industry. There were thousands of Japanese civilian men, women, and children on the island, and they were held in the caves and warrens alongside the troops. As the noose tightened, they were pressed into service to build fighting positions; then they were simply held hostage. They died with the troops. And in the end, they flung themselves from the cliffs into the ocean in front of the eyes of disbelieving American kids who thought until then that they had seen the worst war could expose to them. Mothers took their children with them off the cliffs, and Japanese soldiers who were about to die in useless little rearguard fights used precious bullets on civilian countrymen who could not defend themselves.

Saipan was declared secure on July 9, but fighting persisted for months as the island was scoured for stragglers by its U.S. Army garrison. Some Japanese held out for going on thirty years.

The last-ditch Japanese offensive ran out of steam by noon on July 7, and VAC mounted an immediate and brutally efficient offensive that retook nearly all the lost ground by 1800 hours. *Official USMC Photo*

The last relatively organized Japanese strongpoint on Saipan following the July 7 assault was on Marpi Point, the island's northern extremity. With all but the reinforced 25th Marines squeezed out of the narrowing line, VAC ordered the final offensive. The Japanese troops who were able stood their ground until overwhelmed, and the others went to ground individually or in small groups. *Official USMC Photo*

These Marine light tanks can negotiate rough ground and reach caves in the cliffs with their 37mm guns, but they cannot get close enough to support infantrymen on the heights with any assurance of accuracy. *Official USMC Photo*

A 4th Marine Division rifleman draws a bead on the mouth of a large cave sitting high over the ocean. The only tactically sound way to approach the cave is from above, but that route is likely overseen by yet other caves. In the end, Marines called on warships to rifle shells directly into any cave that could be reached from the sea. Only then were troops lowered to check the results. *Official USMC Photo*

More than nine thousand Japanese civilians—half of them children—fell into American hands alive. Quite often, after using them as laborers and pack animals, Japanese soldiers murdered the civilians with whom they were holed up as either they reached the point of starvation or were about to be overrun. While this mother's face is quite gaunt, the toddlers seem to be unusually well fed. Noncombatants, mounting to more than nine thousand Japanese men, women, and children; about twelve hundred and fifty Korean civilians; and nearly three thousand native Chamorros were winnowed out of groups of captives and placed in guarded stockades where they received ample food and humane treatment. So, for that matter, did about seven hundred and fifty Japanese and Korean military captives. *Official USMC Photo*

Help arrived in the nick of time for this Japanese infant. His father had to be shot dead by Marines when he moved to throw himself and the baby off the cliff and onto the oceanswept rocks below. This was a virtually unique rescue as hundreds of Japanese adults killed themselves and their children in suicide leaps from the cliffs. It broke the hearts of battle-hardened Marines who watched helplessly, at times from only yards away. *Official USMC Photo*

Marine tactical units took part in early mop-up operations after Saipan was declared secure on July 9, 1944, but they were soon replaced by garrison forces, which continued the hunt for bypassed positions and survivors. More than thirty years passed between the end of the battle and the final surrender of a Japanese serviceman on Saipan. *Official USMC Photo*

Official USMC Photo

This Marine 155mm howitzer is one of the types of medium and heavy artillery that pummeled Tinian from southern Saipan in the days leading up to the Tinian invasion. *Official USMC Photo*

2

TINIAN

✮ ✮ ✮ ✮ ✮

July 24–August 1, 1944

J-DAY

THE INVASION AND CAPTURE OF TINIAN was the inevitable extension of the Saipan battle for airfield sites from which the B-29 assault on Japan could be mounted. Following a brief rest and reorganization on Saipan, the 4th Marine Division was launched ashore on J-day, July 24, behind a massive land-based artillery bombardment that had blanketed northern Tinian for days. The invasion beaches were in northwestern Tinian, directly opposite the airfields numbered I and 3, which were well within range of the army-Marine artillery groupment set up in southwestern Saipan. Also in on the bombardment were carrier bombers and fighters, and combat aircraft newly based on Saipan.

The 2d and 8th Marines also were offshore Tinian as the landing force reserve as well as to undertake a feint toward beaches in southwestern Tinian. As at Saipan, the feint was realistic enough to pin Japanese forces to the threatened sector but not enough to draw troops away from the real invasion beaches. Apparently it was good enough to cause the Japanese sector commander to believe that his shore guns had repelled an invasion attempt, and, indeed, a battleship and destroyer were struck by shells that caused numerous casualties.

At 0747, three companies of the 4th Marine Division landed abreast on beaches dubbed White-I and White-2. Although White-I was only 60 yards wide—just wide enough for four amtracs to land abreast—it was to support the entire 24th Marines landing in column of battalions, each in column of companies. White-2, at 160 yards wide, was set aside for the 25th Marines, landing two battalions abreast in columns of companies.

The defense of White-I was negligible but determined, and relatively difficult to overcome due to the narrow landing area.

A carrier-based TBM light bomber orbits over cane fields as fires ignited by bombs and artillery burn on Tinian's Airfield No. 1. *Official U.S. Navy Photo*

The prelanding bombardment was effective enough to knock out this large-caliber naval gun despite its excellent cover and stout protection. This bunker was probably reduced by naval guns fired from directly offshore. The entire island was heavily worked over ahead of the landings to prevent the Japanese from figuring out which beaches would be used. *Official USMC Photo*

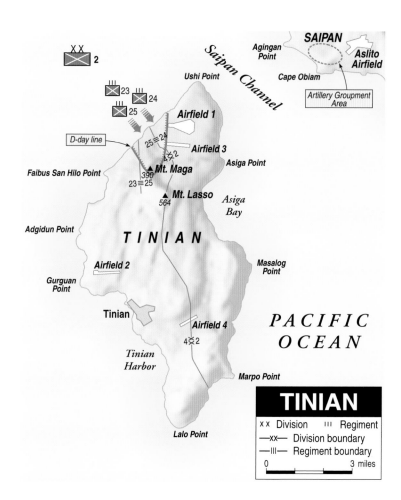

Nevertheless, the opposition was overwhelmed in short order. Behind the beach, 2/24 was harried by mortar fire and Japanese troops holed up in caves, but both types of defenses were smothered by fire, and the advance picked up speed in the direction of the day's phase line. The 1st Battalion, 24th Marines, which began to arrive ashore at 0846, spread left, and 3/24 began to land at 0855 as the regimental reserve.

White-2 was better defended than White-I, and the defenders were ready for battle within two pillboxes and outlying positions that had not been badly mauled by virtue of a prelanding bombardment plan that prized surprise above obliteration. The real surprise, however, was that the initial waves of the 25th Marines landed on rocky ledges bordering White-2, and not on the beach itself. This counterintuitive maneuver caught the Japanese off guard and allowed the entire 25th Marines to get ashore by 0930 without encountering a heavily mined sector at and behind the beach.

Inland, 2/24 easily advanced 1,400 yards to its objective, a line at the edge of Airfield No. 3 that also cut the road to Airfield No. I. To 2/24's left, I/24 ran into strong defenses based in caves

In a bold departure from doctrine and practice, V Amphibious Corps planners selected two very narrow invasion beaches, both impeded by rough terrain on either flank. This certainly was done to fool the Japanese, but the other good reasons for doing so were that both beaches were under a friendly artillery umbrella based in southern Saipan as well as very close to Tinian's two northern airfields. *Official USMC Photos*

As Marine-laden amtracs begin their run on the White beaches, a U.S. Navy cruiser fires at least six of her large main-battery guns at targets on or right behind the shoreline. *Official USMC Photo*

Touchdown! Nearly the first troops ashore, these Marines jump from their amtrac into thigh-deep water and head straight into the fight. *Official USMC Photo*

and dense brush about one thousand yards from White-I. The hitherto rapid advance in the 1/24 zone stalled, but LVT(A)s still in the water fired on the caves, and several flame tanks strove to burn off the underbrush. Thereafter, gun tanks were sent up from the beach as they landed. At 1630 hours, 3/25 was moved up from White-I to close a 400-yard gap that had opened between 1/24 and 2/24, and 1/8 was landed to serve as the 4th Marine Division reserve while the 23d Marines was held offshore as a floating reserve.

On the 4th Division's right, the 25th Marines faced stronger opposition and higher elevations beyond its right flank, from which Japanese observers and artillery had a clear view of the White-2 area. The entire regiment came up well short of its objectives, which were on the first shelf of high ground overlooking the division area.

The first units ashore on Beach White-1 have advanced to a slight rise as reinforcements are pushed ashore in amtracs that dump them and their gear at the surfline to make way for succeeding waves. *Official USMC Photo*

This aerial photo shows amtracs leaving the beach as a follow-on wave bears down with yet more combat troops. Airfield No. 3 is clearly visible in the background, as is a large fire. *Official USMC Photo*

This beachside reinforced concrete pillbox had to be overcome by direct assault. The Japanese defending the White beaches were well entrenched and they fought with great courage, but they were overwhelmed by a greater force of combat-hardened Marines who were backed with a huge array of heavy weapons. *Official USMC Photo*

Marine veterans of hard fighting on Saipan form a skirmish line as they advance warily across a roadway toward a smoke-enshrouded cane field. *Official USMC Photo*

White-2, which was heavily sown with mines and covered by a relatively strong defensive zone, was left to follow-on troops. As soon as the mines were cleared, the 23d Marines was ordered to land on White-2 as proof against an expected counterattack: 2/23 went into the line to the right of the 25th Marines; 1/23 went into a line behind 2/23; and 3/23 was assigned to the division reserve with 1/8.

Advances throughout the beachhead were voluntarily halted at about 1630 to give all the troops time to dig in for the night, and 37mm antitank guns and 2.36-inch bazookas were rushed to the line to be emplaced along likely routes of approach that tanks might use. The entire 4th Tank Battalion—in forty-eight M4 gun tanks and fifteen M3 flame tanks—was ashore by the late afternoon, its tanks fed into the lines as they arrived. By nightfall, all the tanks ashore had been integrated into the defenses that figured so heavily in the J-day planning. Four 75mm pack howitzer battalions (1/14, 2/14, 1/10, and 2/10) and the 4th Marine Division's entire complement of 75mm halftracks also

As the leading combat waves advance inland, follow-on waves aboard amtracs are delivered via a long, orderly line. Mixed in with the Marine amtracs is a battalion of U.S. Army amtracs on loan to V Amphibious Corps. The amtrac at far right is one of them, a new LVT-3, which features a rear ramp so troops can disembark with the bulk of the amtrac between them and enemy fire.
Official USMC Photo

were landed on J-day. Indeed, counting units attached from the 2d Marine Division, the 4th Marine Division controlled more than 15,600 troops ashore by nightfall on July 24.

NIGHT BATTLES

During the first night ashore, the Marine lines were attacked by three large Japanese forces. In the north, at 0200, an estimated six hundred troops from a naval guard force blundered into the defensive line held across the beach by 1/24. The well-prepared Marines opened fire before the Japanese could deploy, and a three-hour blood bath ensued. The next day, 476 Japanese dead were counted in front of the 1/24 line.

In the center, a crack 900-man Japanese infantry battalion infiltrated toward the Marine lines from central Tinian and attacked behind artillery and several tanks pretty much at the juncture of the 24th and 25th Marines, which was inadequately outposted and undermanned. The Japanese attack was easily driven off and thus thought to be a feint. But a second attack on this front made

A Marine M4 medium tank rigged with a fording kit is guided forward through the clutter on a roadway being carved out parallel to the shoreline.
Official USMC Photo

A total of four 75mm pack howitzer battalions were sent ashore on J-day by both the 4th Marine Division's 14th Marines and the 2d Marine Division's 10th Marines. Also, the J-day objective area was covered in its entirety by 105mm and 155mm army and Marine artillery battalions based in southern Saipan.
Official USMC Photo

The aftermath of the fruitless Japanese night attacks against the 4th Marine Division front lines was gruesome to behold but morale-lifting to consider. More than a thousand Imperial Army and Imperial Navy troops sacrificed their lives for nothing rather than to force the Marines to confront them while dug into deep caves and other fighting positions across Tinian's difficult terrain. The Japanese also sacrificed nearly all of their tanks that first night. *Official USMC Photos*

a beeline for Battery A, 1/14, which had to defend itself with its own howitzers and machine guns. A company of 1/8 and a tank platoon counterattacked at 0400 and drove off the surviving Japanese. A third attack into the 25th Marines rear fared no better. In all, an estimated five hundred Japanese died in these attacks.

On the far right, at 0330, the 23d Marines was assaulted directly up the coastal road by six tanks carrying infantrymen, followed by many more infantrymen on foot. In the light of star shells fired by American ships, 75mm halftracks, 37mm antitank guns, and bazookas in the lines of 2/23, directly astride the road, quickly destroyed five tanks and killed the crews and all the infantrymen who rode on them. The sixth tank fled. For all that, veteran troops from three crack infantry battalions assaulted on foot directly into the lines of 2/23 and 2/25, where they were shredded by Marine infantry bolstered by canister-firing antitank

While the two Marines holding this front-line fighting position were overwhelmed and killed, they took at least six of their assailants with them. *Official USMC Photo*

Below: As fresh troops and the accouterments of war poured ashore, the thin but growing stream of casualties was transferred to outbound amtracs and landing craft for the ride to hospital ships and transports with beefed-up medical teams. While casualty treatment ashore got progressively safer as higher and higher medical echelons arrived with better and better field facilities, even better treatment, safer havens, and access to air evacuation from Saipan could be provided more effectively by the ships. *Official USMC Photo*

guns. After dawn 276 Japanese corpses were counted across the 4th Marine Division's left flank, and in all the Japanese wasted at least 1,241 of their troops that night, including nearly seven hundred of their very best.

J+1

The balance of the 8th Marines, the entire 2d Marines, and 2/6 landed on Tinian on July 25, and the rest of the 6th Marines was slated to land on July 26. This was preparation to open a two-division advance down Tinian's long axis as soon as the 4th Marine Division had crossed the entire northern part of the island.

The 4th Division attack on J+1 achieved all of its objectives in the north. On the division's far left, 1/8 attacked northward along the beach, overcame several blocking positions in hard fighting, and stood down several hundred yards north of its starting point. There, 2/8 was fed into the line, facing eastward, to cross the northern reaches of Airfield No. 1 to link up with

continued on page 64

An OY spotter plane from VMO-2 or VMO-4 overflies Marines advancing in a skirmish line across an open cane field. Marine airborne artillery spotters working with Marines on the ground did whatever they could to warn of possible threats and, of course, called artillery, naval gunfire, and air support in aid of the ground troops. *Official USMC Photo*

The broad, open agricultural fields of Tinian were ideal tank country. Marine tanks, which were wholly committed to the support of Marine infantry, were able to bolster and speed the ground advance because of the long reach of their 75mm main guns and the relative invulnerability of their machine guns. Their presence, both as cover and as exemplars of the Marine doctrine of unremitting offense, instilled great confidence in the ranks of vulnerable infantrymen who accompanied them and, in their own way, protected them. *Official USMC Photo*

Advancing along separate axes, the three battalions of the 24th Marines, bolstered by 1/8 and newly landed 2/8, invested Airfield No. 1 and Airfield No. 3 against only limited opposition on J+1, July 25, 1944. *Official USMC Photo*

Stoutly built steel-reinforced hangars, workshops, and air raid shelters were in abundance throughout both of the airfield complexes captured on J+1. Every structure, every pile of rubble, and every fold in the earth had to be painstakingly inspected by teams of dutiful Marines who had every right to be scared stiff and trigger-happy as they went about this most dangerous of combat chores. These Marines actually persuaded the occupants of this shelter—probably aircraft technicians—to surrender.
Official USMC Photo

Through all of J+1, the 25th Marines was faced with a tough, climbing fight to secure Mount Maga from enemy troops determined to hold on to high ground with a direct view of the entire northern—Marine-held—end of Tinian. First there was an arduous climb that even these veterans of hilly Saipan found difficult. *Official USMC Photo*

The stiff resistance on Mount Maga could not be overcome with infantry weapons alone, not even when wielded by brave veterans. Tanks were called in as soon as a road up the mountain was located, and flamethrowers also were sent into the battle for the heights. *Official USMC Photo*

Continued from page 61

1/24. The juncture was effected halfway across the airfield. In the meantime, 3/24 attacked eastward against negligible opposition, then turned south to support 2/24 as the latter crossed Airfield No. 3. In effect, the Marine line both pivoted around Airfield No. 1 and expanded to accommodate a zone for the 2d Marine Division to the left of the 4th Marine Division.

In the 4th Division center, the 25th Marines had ended J-day well short of its objectives atop Mount Maga. On J+1, while 2/25 manned a base of fire in the center, the rest of the regiment opened a double envelopment, 3/25 on the left and 1/25 on the right. In the 1/25 zone, the infantry was driven back by heavy fire, but tanks drove to the peak once a newly discovered road was cleared of mines. At first, 1/25 was unable to follow, but in due

A flamethrower in action against a Japanese defensive emplacement. *Official USMC Photo*

course the Japanese positions were reduced by 81mm mortar fire, and the infantry joined the tanks in the early afternoon. A seesaw battle ensued as the two sides dueled for the heights, but the tanks prevailed, and 1/25 continued around the mountain to link up with 3/25. For its part, 3/25 faced delay after delay in the face of tough opposition despite reinforcement by tanks and flamethrower teams as well as artillery and naval gunfire support. In the meantime, elements of the 23d Marines came up on the right, took out positions in its zone that had stopped 3/25, and 3/25 leaped forward to link up with 1/25. Indeed, the entire 4th Division achieved all of its goals by 1700 at remarkably light cost to the assault battalions.

Japanese artillery either emplaced on the heights facing the Marine advance, or observed from these heights, was active and accurate throughout the day. A direct hit on the 1/14 fire direction center claimed the lives of the battalion commander and eight others, and Seabees building a pier at Beach White-2 sustained losses in another shelling. Air strikes, naval gunfire, and counterbattery fire apparently destroyed several Japanese guns.

THE CORPS ADVANCE

On July 26, J+2, the 2d Marine Division resumed control of the 8th Marines and took over a sector to the left of the 4th Marine Division. Also, 1/6, 3/6, the 2d Tank Battalion, and other units came ashore to complete the 2d Division order of battle.

continued on page 68

A great deal of the VAC advance across central and southern Tinian was accomplished by troops plodding alongside tanks over heavily cultivated flatlands. The broad, flat vistas helped the Marines see what lay ahead and plan their approaches accordingly, but they also provided the defenders with clear shots at advancing Marines.
Official USMC Photos

In addition to gun tanks, Marine infantry units often had direct support from flame tanks as well as M3 tank destroyers, whose 75mm guns were the same weapon with which the gun tanks were equipped. The advance across the cultivated areas of central and southern Tinian represented the first of just two mobile Marine Corps campaigns of the Pacific War (the other was northern Okinawa). The tracked and semi-tracked combat vehicles were especially important here, because they could keep pace with the fast-moving infantry. *Official USMC Photos*

Continued from page 65

The 8th Marines crossed Airfield No. 1 and stood on the eastern coast by 1140, then passed into division reserve. To the left, covering Tinian's northern point, the 2d Marines was committed to the fight at dawn, and it reached the eastern coast by 1230. There it redressed its line to face south in anticipation of a two-division drive down Tinian's long axis. The 6th Marines quietly moved into the southward-facing 2d Division line, tied in on the left with the 2d Marines and on the right with the 25th Marines.

The seaward flanks of both advancing Marine divisions were often guarded by warships that could lend fire support in seconds. Lookouts aboard these ships also located numerous cliffside caves that the Marines on land could not see for themselves, and, of course, the naval guns helped the Marines clear these caves. *Official USMC Photo*

In securing Tinian Town, the island's largest settlement by far, elements of the 4th Marine Division just flattened the place. *Official USMC Photo*

On the 4th Division right, the 23d Marines rapidly advanced past Point Faibus San Hilo and stood down to wait for all the other regiments to draw abreast. The 25th Marines, from atop Mount Maga, advanced southward in the direction of Mount Lasso, the greatly feared fulcrum of the island's defenses. Unbelievably, the Japanese had abandoned the strategic heights in the night, so the 25th Marines both occupied the peak and ringed the heights to the south. The 24th Marines was squeezed out of the V Amphibious Corps front and placed in reserve. Thus, by the end of J+2, four Marine regiments stood in line completely across the island from the west across Mount Lasso, then northeast and east to Asiga Point.

As VAC units advanced south, they hit a number of high plateaus, where the fight was pretty much in the hands of unsupported infantrymen who had to climb quite high over trackless hillsides just to locate enemy troops—and Saipan's civilians—who had pretty much gone to ground in the broken wilderness. *Official USMC Photos*

It is probable that a large ammunition dump has been located by artillery fire. Note the deep, clear vistas of the southern half of Tinian these 4th Division Marines have at their feet. *Official USMC Photo*

All of the infantry and support units had entered the fight on Tinian in reduced states because no replacements had been available during or after the Saipan battle, but each was battle-tested, tough, and sure of itself. They had won the strategic battle in only three days. All they had to do from then on was actually clear the lower half of Tinian. To help do this—because Marine gains were running beyond the range of Saipan-based artillery—3/14 landed its 105mm howitzers on Tinian on J+2, and other artillery units on Saipan were told to pack for the same brief ride.

This enterprising Marine 75mm pack howitzer crew broke its weapon down into its four portable components, manpacked them to the heights, reassembled the howitzer, lashed it down so the recoil would not send it tumbling out of control, and repeatedly fired it straight into the open maw of a large cave. This is one of the few documented occasions in which the manpackable pack howitzer was packed over rough terrain by men alone. *Official USMC Photo*

TINIAN SECURED

The VAC attack down the long axis of Tinian was rapid and efficient—costly to the Japanese and much less costly to the Americans. By July 31, Airfield No. 2 and Airfield No. 4 were in American hands, and the two Marine divisions had driven to the high, jumbled plateaus that characterized the southernmost portion of the island. The fighting turned extremely tough here, partly because of the steep cave-studded terrain, but also because the defenders had become so concentrated. Great effort was expended to induce Japanese and Korean civilians to surrender, and more than eight thousand answered the call, thus obviating a repeat of the thousands of needless civilian deaths on Saipan. Here also, for the first time in the Pacific War, significant numbers of Japanese servicemen also surrendered.

Following the horror of the mass suicides on Saipan, if there was even a faint hope that the occupants of a cave or dugout could be cajoled out without a fight, interpreters were brought up to do the talking. Often, an offer of food, water, or cigarettes was enough to turn the key, for the civilian and military occupants of the caves were often dying of hunger or thirst, or simply going through nicotine withdrawal. *Official USMC Photo*

In one of the last battles on Tinian involving organized Japanese troops, a 2d Marine Division unit gruesomely killed the occupants of this machine gun bunker, on the island's southern tip, probably with a flame tank that might have detonated stored ammunition. *Official USMC Photo*

The island was declared secure on August 1, but mopping up continued for weeks and even months. The death toll in the two Marine divisions was 317 killed and 1,550 wounded, and an estimated five thousand Japanese troops died on Tinian.

Thousands of Japanese, Korean, and native Chamorro noncombatants hid out in caves in the Tinian escarpment as Marines cleared the area of Japanese fighters. While more than eight thousand civilians were saved, many, many others were held hostage by soldiers, as they had been on Saipan, and thus thousands also died, many by starvation. Painstaking cave-by-cave clearing operations were conducted by the 8th Marines well into October, but some Japanese troops hid out for as long as three decades.

The 2d Marine Division remained on Saipan, where it made good its losses and was reorganized under a new table of organization. The 4th Marine Division was shipped back to Hawaii for the same treatment.

Japanese combatants were separated from Japanese, Korean, and native Chamorro civilians, who were separated from one another, but everyone on Tinian who wasn't an American went behind barbed wire. The civilians were not so much imprisoned as brought together so they could be efficiently identified, fed, and medically treated. The occupants of this camp are probably Japanese or Korean civilians. Note how rudimentary the stockade barrier is. *Official USMC Photo*

It is sometimes difficult to remember that most Marines who shouldered the fighting in World War II were in their late teens or early twenties—just plain American kids who killed because they had to but who reverted to their basic good nature between the gruesome chores of war. *Official USMC Photo*

A U.S. Navy cruiser fires at a shore target on Guam from point-blank range. *Official U.S. Navy Photo*

3

GUAM

★ ★ ★ ★ ★

July 21–August 11, 1944

INVASION DELAYED

W-DAY, THE INVASION OF GUAM, was to have followed the June 15 invasion of Saipan by three days. It was delayed, however, by the Battle of the Philippine Sea, when the transports were ordered away from the area and the 27th Infantry Division, set aside as the reserve for the entire Marianas campaign, was sent ashore on Saipan. This forced the commanders to designate part of the Guam invasion force as the temporary reserve for Saipan and to scramble to bring up another army division from Hawaii, an operation that took time and involved the well-trained but inexperienced and unbriefed 77th Infantry Division. W-day was set back to July 21.

The intervening month was put to good use obliterating targets that could be observed from the sea or the air, including virtually every fixed artillery piece on Guam. But the focus of the prolonged preparatory bombardments allowed the Japanese to mass at precisely the points at which the invasion forces were to land.

The beaches selected for the landings were not as good as other beaches around the island. Wide reefs rising almost to the surface necessitated the early seizure of suitable port facilities from which the invasion force could be sustained, and the best of these were in a marginal landing area from which the island's main airfield also was accessible.

In the end, given the relentless factors from which such solutions were derived, the invasion force of five Marine infantry regiments— the 3d Marine Division (3d, 9th, and 21st Marines) and the 1st Provisional Marine Brigade (4th and 22d Marines)—had to be split, and the two forces had to land *5 miles apart* on narrow beaches impinged and dominated by high, broken hill country. The main reason for

A large conflagration erupts—perhaps in an ammunition dump—as rounds fired by U.S. Navy warships strike Guam's shoreline in the run-up to the invasion. *Official U.S. Navy Photo*

This is one of the many Japanese large-caliber seacoast guns that were put out of action ahead of the landing. It is believed that no large-caliber weapons were able to oppose the W-day landings or subsequent Marine and army advances on Guam. *Official USMC Photo*

landing the landing forces so far apart also was bound up in the inexorable calculus of war. While the 1st Brigade and at least one army regiment went after Orote Airfield, port facilities on Orote Peninsula, and the southern third of the large island, the 3d Marine Division was to seize the northern two-thirds of Guam. This was because Guam had been selected as a forward base for the B-29 program. Thus the invasion plan for Guam favored the early seizure of suitable sites for three large airfields, and all such sites were in northern and central Guam, in the 3d Marine Division's zone of operations. A landing farther to the north would have allowed the 3d Marine Division to employ better landing beaches closer to two of the three airfield sites, but that option was set aside in favor of landing the division as near to the brigade as possible without compromising its strategic mission. Before striking north to seize ground for the B-29 bases, the division was to link up with the brigade along a continuous, defensible front, the so-called Final Beachhead Line. It was

This beachside pillbox in the 1st Provisional Marine Brigade zone was destroyed by a direct hit ahead of the landings. *Official USMC Photo*

anticipated that the linkup and thus the start of the northern drive could be achieved within a day or two.

W-DAY

The final preparatory bombardment of the landing beaches was ferocious but flawed. From close in and afar, dozens of ships, from rocket-firing LCI(R) gunboats to battleships, pounded the cliffs and hills overlooking the landing beaches north and south of the Orote Peninsula. The gunfire and bombs from scores and scores of navy carrier planes scorched the earth and destroyed virtually all of the fixed antiboat defenses that had survived the month-long bombardment. And the detonations of those bombs and shells certainly addled the brains of most of the Japanese troops deployed in the invasion zone. But it is doubtful if all that fire actually *killed* very many of the defenders, for the month-long run-up to the invasion had given the Japanese time to dig secure bunkers and caves on the largely unreachable *reverse* slopes of the many high hills overlooking the landing beaches.

What worked is that the landing waves assigned to both sets of beaches got ashore intact and with few casualties. A number of cunningly emplaced and beautifully camouflaged antiboat guns

Marines leap from the troop compartment of this amtrac to seek cover on the sandy beach. *Official USMC Photo*

After seeking cover at the water's edge from which they can assess the situation around them, Marine infantrymen on all the invasion beaches sorted themselves out and began to advance inland. *Official USMC Photos*

and machine guns destroyed or disabled a significant number of Marine amtracs, which were essential for the landing, for not one landing craft could get across the reef. Most of these defensive weapons were destroyed in short order by hovering navy fighter-bombers or destroyers and cruisers stationed off the beaches.

The 3d Marine Division landed its three infantry regiments abreast between Asan Point and Adelup Point, north of Orote Peninsula, on Guam's western shore. And the 1st Provisional Marine Brigade landed its two infantry regiments abreast between Bangi Point and the town of Agat, at the base of Orote Peninsula. Several amtracs were hit by the antiboat fire, and there were casualties, but most tractors that were lost that morning were put out of commission when their treads were chewed up by the coral.

The lead waves, which were ashore in good order by 0832 hours, formed up, ready to drive on their objectives. But as they did, the defenders shook off the effects of the bombardment, emerged from their reverse-slope burrows, and put up such fierce resistance from the heights that the planned drives to widen the beachhead and link the division with the brigade were stalled in their tracks. In some cases the invaders drove a hundred yards inland from the water line, but no farther.

These Marines were killed on the beach when the trench they were using for cover took a direct artillery or mortar hit. *Official USMC Photo*

Already briefed to drive for the heights, 3/3, on the 3d Marine Division's left flank, *had* to do so to save itself from deadly plunging fire. The battalion's assigned objective was Chonito Cliff, a high eminence that ran to the water line and thus completely restricted access to the interior as well as the shoreline to the northeast. Fortunately, several companies of 3/3 and several medium tanks were able to advance in the protection of a draw, and the height was in Marine hands by noon. But when 3/3 tried to advance from Chonito Cliff, it was stopped by fire from a high ridge in the neighboring 1/3 zone that 1/3 could in no way overcome. Indeed, 1/3 also was pinned by fire from this prickly ridge, and it could not advance without sustaining many casualties.

Having anticipated big problems taking Chonito Cliff, the regimental plan had to be altered on the fly to account for the deadly delay encountered by 1/3. First, 2/3, the regimental reserve, was committed and sent around the Japanese-held ridge, but this did not relieve pressure on 1/3, whose Company A could not advance without drawing withering fire from the heights. In a frustrating second attack that nearly claimed the heights, Company A's Captain Geary Bundschu was killed, and the ridge was named for him.

As amtracs carry follow-on waves across the reef in the 3d Marine Division zone, first-wave troops who have already reached the first level of high ground overlooking the beaches establish overwatch positions and re-form to push ahead to the next objective line. *Official USMC Photo*

As soon as possible, Marine communicators established a wide communications net by which senior commanders could control the efforts of large units ashore. Shown here is a TBS (Talk Between Ships) radio that typically linked battalions and regiments. *Official USMC Photo*

But the 3d Marine Division's problems did not revolve around one rugged spot. Virtually the entire division was hemmed in by well-defended ridges and hills that dominated most of the packed landing beaches. The day ended with the 3d Marine Division in possession of the beach, Chonito Cliff, and not much else. The 3d Marines was not even in physical contact with the adjacent 21st Marines. Only from the 9th Marines sector, on the division right, was there a report of success: the regiment had landed in good order and taken all its W-day objectives, but at the cost to the regiment of 231 killed and wounded, including a battalion commander wounded and 2 company commanders killed.

Landing into better terrain, the 1st Brigade had an easier time getting itself established on or near its W-day objectives,

continued on page 84

As the battle moved inland, follow-on waves that arrived in landing craft were eventually dropped as close to the beach as possible. Many amtracs were sidelined, even on W-day, because of damage to their tracks by sharp coral. In the end there were not enough amtracs, nor enough time to fill them, as more troops were needed ashore to fight. *Official USMC Photo*

Marine infantry companies brought their own artillery ashore: 60mm mortars, which were set up right behind the front-line riflemen. They could fire high-explosive shrapnel or smoke rounds. *Official USMC Photo*

Orote Field, in the 1st Brigade zone, had been the focal point of several big air clashes during the so-called Marianas Turkey Shoot in mid-June. Many Imperial Navy aircraft downed over Orote Field littered the 1st Brigade battle zone. *Official USMC Photo*

Typical of fast-paced amphibious assaults, where strengthening and supplying a newly established beachhead are paramount, the clutter builds up rapidly on the beach, and that impedes the progress to the front of vitally needed reinforcements, such as these 1st Brigade tanks. Note that a wounded Marine is being treated in the center of the beach, and that many of the Marines shown seem to be killing time gabbing with others or just watching the world go by. *Official USMC Photo*

Saving Lives

This Marine artilleryman has just been wounded by shrapnel from a round fired by a Japanese light artillery piece. He is being treated by navy hospital corpsmen with the help of his buddies. They are all very lucky that the Japanese shell did not detonate the ready ammunition seen in two places on the left side of this photo. *Official USMC Photo*

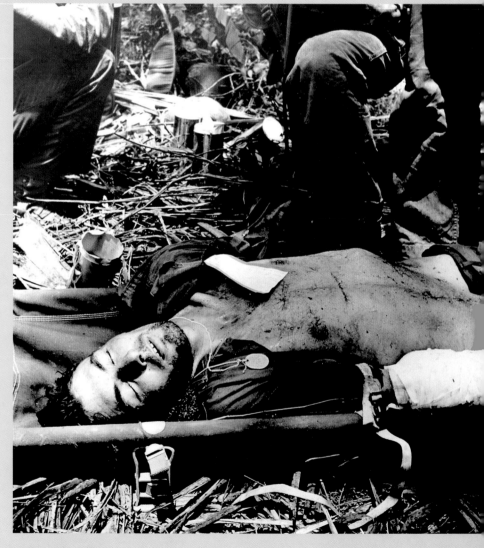

From the front lines, the wounded are concentrated at the nearest aid station, usually manned by a battalion or regimental surgical team. This front-line aid station will probably be moved inland as the beachhead is made deeper, and it will probably move into reasonably well-equipped tents. At aid stations like this, corpsmen and surgeons fight shock, suture wounds, and stabilize fractures before dispatching the injured man to a ship offshore. As the battalion aid station and the battle lines move farther out, transfers might be made to a much larger and better-equipped facility ashore. *Official USMC Photo*

For all that a battalion aid station in combat operated in extremis, excellent, life-giving care was the norm. The Marine shown here has a burned or broken right arm swathed in bandages and at least two long rows of sutures form lines across his sternum. If he survives, he owes it all to quick-acting front-line corpsmen and doctors. *Official USMC Photo*

As soon as possible after being stabilized and perhaps taking on blood or plasma, the wounded man is evacuated from the island aboard any conveyance available. The rapid sequence to evacuation from the island is to clear space and personnel to help others, to guard against infection in relatively unsanitary surroundings, and because aid stations are not immune from taking fire from Japanese artillery or being overrun in Japanese attacks. The amphibious vehicle shown here is a DUKW amphibian truck. *Official USMC Photo*

This W-day photo shows casualties being treated aboard a coast guard LCVP by a coast guard surgeon. Several LCVPs and other landing craft were equipped and manned to serve as floating aid stations until battalion aid stations could be safely established in the expanding beachhead. As to safety, this LCVP has its bow ramp down because the device has taken a direct hit from a Japanese mortar round. The crewmen at right are trying to figure out how to get the ramp up. If they can't, the aid station will be cross-decked to the LCVP at right. *Official U.S. Coast Guard Photo*

All medical evacuees were hoisted aboard hospital ships or transports designated as hospital ships because their medical staffs had been amply beefed up. Most of the wounded made the journey to rear bases aboard ship, but some whose injuries required care by specialists at hospitals ashore could be run up to Saipan and flown to large rear bases with the right kind of medical facilities, or even all the way back to the United States. It happens that the two evacuees seen here are Japanese soldiers, who have and will receive the same good care as wounded and injured American servicemen. *Official USMC Photo*

Continued from page 80

although not without heavy casualties in some units. Despite the brigade's success, the brigade commander decided to draw on his reserve, an army infantry battalion. Because of heavy losses among Marine amtracs during the initial landing, the army battalion was forced to wade to the beach from the reef. When the brigade commander ordered the rest of the reserve army regiment ashore late in the day, a series of communications foul-ups kept it from landing until the wee hours, and then it arrived in too disorganized a state to be of any immediate use. There were also problems getting the brigade's artillery ashore.

NIGHT MOVES

The bulk of the Japanese infantry regiment facing the brigade mounted an ill-advised, desultory, disorganized, and ultimately unsuccessful counterattack during the night. Hundreds of Japanese soldiers died for no good reason, and any hope the Japanese island commander might have had of holding the brigade to minimal gains was dashed in that foolish act. There were American casualties and other losses, but not enough to justify the

Men at war often go without sleep for a day or more at a time, but they became habituated to the long periods of stress-driven wakefulness interspersed with brief, deeply restful catnaps at every possible opportunity. This Marine is ready for a fight at a moment's notice. *Official USMC Photo*

In the 3d Marine Division zone, all directions seemed to be up. *Official USMC Photo*

The higher elements of the 3d Marine Division climbed, the longer the way down it was for the wounded and injured. Here, guylines have been rigged and manned to gingerly lower a wounded Marine to better medical care than he can receive on the front line. *Official USMC Photo*

immolation of two of the three Japanese infantry battalions facing the southern beachhead. Guam's defenders had gone into W-day facing little hope of turning back the American tide, and they faced their second dawn of battle with *no* hope of holding the island. Thereafter, while the southern half of Guam was not abandoned by the Japanese, it was open for the taking—at a price.

Quite the opposite happened in the 3d Marine Division zone. The Japanese used the night to plug holes and otherwise strengthen their defenses. There were counterattacks here, too, during the night, and several Japanese battalions were chewed to bits, but the majority of the defenders stayed where they were or repositioned themselves to better advantage. The ground favored the defenders, and the Japanese here used it wisely. And then they used the entire second day, July 22, to wear down the Marines by grinding action.

THE 3d MARINE DIVISION'S FIGHT

The second day's fighting in the 3d Marine Division zone still centered on Bundschu Ridge, in 1/3's zone. There were many

Most of the daylight fighting in the high hills and ridges of the 3d Marine Division zone took place at long range between small groups of combatants isolated from larger friendly forces. *Official USMC Photo*

Marine attacks but few gains. The adjacent 21st Marines had to sit pretty still for most of the day, because an advance in its zone would expose the center regiment to flanking fire from Bundschu Ridge and other, unreachable, heights. The 21st Marines was able to extend its control over a broader reach in some directions, but it was not able to gain direct physical contact with the adjacent 3d Marines because the twisted, hilly terrain was impenetrable beyond imagination. In contrast, the 9th Marines, on the division right, was able to eliminate most of the defenders in its zone and advance to flat ground, but the regiment's progress toward even broader vistas was slowed when the remaining defenders in its zone skillfully stood fast in numerous little ad hoc strongpoints that had to be cleared with painstaking care. At length, 2/9 captured the old Piti Navy Yard, a major divisional objective that was to become one of the island's key supply points.

The 3d Marine Division's plan of action for July 23 was to physically link the 3d and 21st Marine regiments. This plan was immensely aided by fruitless Japanese counterattacks

Mortars and howitzers saved many a day in the hilly country. Guided by front-line observers, they were able to put their high-angle rounds right on top of Japanese positions built into the rear slopes of many hills. *Official USMC Photo*

during the night that weakened the defense. One defending battalion destroyed itself making piecemeal suicide attacks that had no effect on the Marines.

On the morning of July 23, the 3d Marines continued to move upon the high ground and gullies that had all but stymied its planned advance on two previous days. First, 1/3 was reinforced—to an effective strength of 160—and sent back to take Bundschu Ridge behind a massive air, naval, and artillery bombardment. Almost as soon as 1/3 jumped off, and 2/3 also moved on Bundschu Ridge, the objective fell without a fight; the Japanese had abandoned this defensive key point, although the entire day had to be spent cleaning out hot spots on the ridge. Meanwhile, the 3d and 21st Marines attempted to gain firm physical contact in that area, but they could not; the complexity of the terrain simply could not be overcome.

The Japanese put their main effort during the day on keeping 3/3 from exploiting its position on Chonito Cliff. With Bundschu Ridge in Marine hands, the division's left-flank battalion appeared to be free to expand to its next objective, Fonte Plateau, and 3/3 managed to advance about halfway to this objective, albeit at great cost.

The 21st Marines spent July 23 trying to link up with the 3d Marines on its left and attempting to make modest gains in the center, mostly for the sake of tying down Japanese troops who might otherwise have been shifted to the 9th or 3d Marines' zones. Although the defense in its zone was sporadic, the 9th Marines spent the day merely improving its positions. The division reserve, 1/21, was sent to bolster the 3d Marines, and 2/9 was withdrawn from the 9th Marines zone to be the division reserve.

Far from internalizing the lessons of the previous two nights—that night attacks made in the open simply fritter away the lives of the troops—Guam's Japanese commander had been planning through the day to mount a major, all-out counterattack that he hoped would drive the vastly stronger 3d Marine Division into the sea. Because the Japanese communications system had been destroyed by bombs and shells, the attacks were fragmented and piecemeal, and they were easily turned back by Marines holding excellent defensive positions as well as by sustained artillery and naval gunfire laid to perfection on known assembly areas and routes of approach. Once again, many Japanese died for absolutely no good reason.

Japanese tanks were fairly commonplace in the lower, flatter 1st Brigade zone, but only as long as they lasted. The Japanese had no effective tank doctrine, so they were unable to use tanks effectively against American infantry, and even their best tanks were in no way built to stand up to modern antitank guns or, for sure, the 75mm cannon with which American medium tanks were armed. The Japanese tank in the second photo has been destroyed—not by gunfire, but by the impact of the blade attached to the Marine Sherman. *Official USMC Photos*

Flamethrowers really came into their own during the three Marianas battles. They were deployed in abundance for the first time, and by then the Marine Corps had worked out an adequate doctrine for their use. Shown here, a squad of Marines gratefully weathers the heat, which all hands know is better than going after this pillbox with small arms and explosives. *Official USMC Photo*

The fighting was heavy in the 3d Marine Division's zone on July 24, but the objectives, and thus the gains, were modest. All three regiments continued to improve their positions as necessary, and 2/21 was finally able to effect an adequate link with the 3d Marines. By 1400, for the first time since landing, the 3d Marine Division held a continuous line, albeit well short of its objectives for the fourth day on Guam. An attempt also was made by 9th Marines patrols to contact the 1st Provisional Marine Brigade, but the effort fell well short of the objective, although one patrol advanced quite far into a zone that had clearly been abandoned by its defenders.

THE 1st PROVISIONAL MARINE BRIGADE'S FIGHT

In general, the 1st Provisional Marine Brigade—bolstered to divisional strength with the addition of a U.S. Army infantry regiment on W-day—did better in its zone of action from July 22 to July 24. But the terrain and the circumstances were different, so there is no real point of comparison. On July 22, the brigade concentrated on expanding to the north, toward the base of Orote Peninsula. There were steep, heavily wooded slopes to overcome in some sectors, and the going was slow, particularly as the defense became more concentrated, but the gains were nonetheless substantial. The army regiment took its objectives on the flat shoreside flank to the south, but 1/4 had a very hard time navigating up the steep, wooded, well-defended slopes of dominant Mount Alifan in the face of plunging fire. The Japanese eventually abandoned the heights, and 1/4 completed the climb. Also, 3/4 made good its objectives for the day, and the worst problems the 22d Marines faced in its zone to the north was getting enough supplies up from the beach to sustain its advance into jumbled, sparsely defended terrain. Tanks and LVT(A)s had to be employed to help 1/22 advance down the coast, but the defenses there were overcome. In the meantime, most of the III Amphibious

By this stage of the Pacific War, Marine tanks and infantry worked well as an integrated team. Note that most of the infantrymen in this photo use the tanks as a barrier between themselves and the foliage they suspect is a harbor for Japanese troops. Note also that these Shermans have their main guns deployed to cover both sides of the trail. If Japanese open fire, the tank covering that side of the trail will blast them with its main gun and coaxial machine gun, which will stun and hurt the enemy as well as point out their positions to the infantry, who will keep up their end of the bargain by protecting the tanks from being overwhelmed by a rush of enemy troops. The 55-gallon drums carry drinking water for the infantrymen. *Official USMC Photo*

Corps (IIIAC) artillery group was landed in the brigade beachhead during the day, as was some of the 77th Division's artillery.

On July 23, the army regiment reached its sector on the Final Beachhead Line, and the 22d Marines all but sealed off the neck of Orote Peninsula in the face of a determined, organized defensive effort that inflicted more than a hundred casualties. While these advances were proceeding, the bulk of the 77th Division, less one regiment held in corps reserve, was concentrated in the 1st Brigade zone. Elements of the 4th Marines were replaced on the inland flank late in the day by elements of the fresh army regiment, and the 4th Marines withdrew to positions from which it could attack into Orote Peninsula.

The 1st Brigade's July 24 attack was preceded by a massive air, artillery, and naval bombardment, especially in the 22d Marines zone, across the neck of Orote Peninsula. When 1/22 jumped off, however, the Japanese responded with heavy artillery, mortar, and machine gun fire. Marine M4 tanks with the lead company destroyed five Japanese tanks that tried to thwart the attack, and 75mm guns aboard these M4s also neutralized log and even concrete pillboxes that stood in the way of 1/22's advance. Close-in 20mm and 40mm flanking fire from LCI(G) gunboats also contributed to 1/22's success, as did direct and enfilade 5-inch fire from a destroyer. When 1/22 had advanced well into the Japanese line, 3/22 mounted a flanking attack that rolled up much of the remaining Japanese defensive position. A major Japanese strongpoint was overcome by 3/22. On the regimental right, 2/22 rolled into its attack late, but it made important gains throughout the afternoon. By day's end, 1/22 and 2/22 were on their day's objectives—the line from which Orote Peninsula would be assaulted—and 3/22 was nearly there. Also, the 4th Marines, fully relieved by an army regiment, went into 1st Brigade reserve behind or even with the 22d Marines.

A NEW PLAN

The last army infantry regiment was landed in the 1st Brigade zone on July 24 as the corps reserve. Equally important was that the ship-to-shore movement of supplies into both beachheads was so well in hand as to be characterized as routine, and a major water point was established at a spring in the 3d Marine Division's zone.

Under the original IIIAC plan, the 3d Marine Division and the 1st Provisional Marine Brigade were to have been in contact and in complete control of the corps' Final Beachhead Line by the evening of July 24. By then, however, the brigade was still marginally short of its objective (even after having been reinforced by an army force greater than its own strength), and the 3d Marine Division was well short of its landing-phase goals. Moreover, the two beachheads were not yet joined. Thus the brigade was given an extra day, July 25, to seal off Orote Peninsula and prepare for its attack into that well-defended feature, and the 3d Marine Division was ordered to continue its move on the Final Beachhead Line in its zone and to make contact with the brigade. The 77th Division was to expand the southern beachhead to the Final Beachhead Line and prepare to extend itself over the southern third of Guam (formerly a 1st Brigade objective).

Relying largely on supporting artillery, air, gunboats, and naval gunfire, the 22d Marines advanced into defensive sectors that had clearly been stiffened during the night. (In fact, guns emplaced in the 3d Marine Division's zone had fired on illuminated Japanese landing barges bringing troops to Orote Peninsula through the night from other areas of Guam.) The 22d Marines did seal off Orote Peninsula, but it was clear by the end of the day that both regiments of the 1st Brigade would be needed to grind into a concentrated defensive zone extending well back into the peninsula. On the bright side, patrols from 2/22 made contact with patrols from the 9th Marines on ground the Japanese had abandoned. Firm contact between the 1st Brigade and the 3d Marine Division could not yet be sealed, but it was clear that joining the Marine commands would not be a major problem once enough troops were sent into the gap.

The 3d Marine Division continued to take ground in its zone, but advances remained limited, in part because of the jumbled terrain and in part because the Japanese put up a lot of resistance on certain features that, as it turned out, they were trying to hold as jumping-off points for an all-out ground offensive the Japanese commander hoped would drive the 3d Marine Division into the sea. The Japanese did hold these points, but at such great cost as to render some units ineffective for the upcoming attack.

During the morning of July 25, 2/9 moved into the 3d Marines' zone to relieve 1/3, which was fought out, and it secured large parts of Fonte Plateau during the day. Also, large numbers of Marine tanks were committed for the first time in the division zone, because there was finally ground on the division's front on which they could operate. Their effect on the fighting was profound. For all that, the division's line in the 3d and 21st Marines zones was jumbled and broken by day's end—a factor of the terrain and irregular advances from one battalion zone to the next. The result was that many units had to form battalion-size strongpoints on suitably defensible features. The 9th Marines reached its day's limited objectives on better ground without much trouble, but the regiment was held up by the need to remain in step with the 3d and 21st Marines. Nevertheless, the 21st and 9th Marines had lost contact by nightfall.

THE LAST COUNTERATTACK

The all-out Japanese attack began at 2330 hours on July 25. Its main weight fell precisely on the gap that had developed and remained open between 3/21 and 1/9. The rather fragmented 3d Marines also was hit hard. Artillery and naval gunfire were placed on the advancing Japanese, who nevertheless closed on many Marine positions in the dark. There were some close calls, particularly where the Japanese outnumbered the defenders, but the attack was uncoordinated once it began, and opportunities to

The sheer desperation of the Japanese position on Guam by July 25 is amply illustrated by this weapon—a bayonet lashed to a bamboo pole—which was policed up from the battlefield in the wake of the final, all-out night attack. *Official USMC Photo*

A .30-caliber medium machine gun has been set in to provide overhead cover for troops advancing across flat terrain toward a distant ridgeline. Note that the gunner has a pair of binoculars ready at hand. *Official USMC Photo*

overwhelm some Marine positions were lost by the inability of the Japanese to concentrate their forces. Indeed, all the Japanese tanks assigned to the attack became lost, and none reached the front. American artillery and naval gunfire was effective against the Japanese routes of approach and assembly areas, but it could not be fired into areas where the Japanese and Americans were intermingled. Repeated Japanese infantry attacks failed to dislodge any of the Marine units. Marine tanks made a critical difference in some zones, particularly in support of 2/9, whose perimeter on Fonte Plateau was strongly attacked seven times during the night. The tanks became particularly effective at dawn, when visibility increased to the decisive advantage of the defenders. Of course,

continued on page 98

The final night assault signaled to Marine commanders that it was time to put the advance out of the grimly expanded beachheads into high gear. Against waning opposition that still remained organized and heroic in some places, the Marines and their army cohorts moved out to secure the rest of Guam. Here, 1st Marine Brigade troops and medium tanks advance confidently and rapidly into Orote Peninsula across relatively open ground. *Official USMC Photo*

A Marine rifle squad follows closely behind a medium tank in this extremely close-in terrain. *Official USMC Photo*

The Sherman has just fired a 75mm armor-piercing round at a Japanese pillbox dead ahead. Marine infantrymen hidden in deep cover will assault the pillbox as soon as the unit leader thinks the tank has done all it can to soften or silence the position. *Official USMC Photo*

These 1st Brigade engineers are inspecting the contents of a manmade cave in a steep-sided gully preparatory to blowing the whole thing up. *Official USMC Photo*

This 3d Division sharpshooter has armed himself with a BAR to take on a Japanese sniper who has been spotted firing from a lair a thousand feet down and across from the Marine's hillside position. Used properly and fired one shot at a time, the BAR could be an excellent long-range sniper rifle. *Official USMC Photo*

The port town of Sumay, on the shore of Orote Peninsula, was virtually flattened in heavy fighting. Before Guam fell to the Japanese on December 10, 1941, Sumay had been the center of service life on Guam, because naval and Marine units were based there. *Official USMC Photo*

It's been a long road back. These Marines, who have fought their way across thousands of miles of Japanese-held territory, finally clear the account with brother Marines who were forced to surrender Guam to a superior Japanese force only four days into the Pacific War. Officiating at a solemn July 29, 1944, flag-raising ceremony attended by several Marines who had spent tours at Marine Barracks, Sumay, is IIIAC commander Major General Roy Geiger (in khaki uniform just to the left of the flagpole). The national colors are going up on the same flagpole from which they were struck on December 10, 1941. *Official USMC Photo*

The fight for Guam is nearing resolution. The Japanese light tank, which Marine tankers have stopped to inspect, is one of the last to be encountered on the island.
Official USMC Photo

Marine riflemen sprint down the length of a wall that was only recently held—on the other side—by Japanese these same Marines probably attempted to dislodge with fire. *Official USMC Photo*

Guam's capital, Agana, fell into Marine hands on July 31 following a hard fight that reduced the town to rubble. The entire town had to be combed for Japanese who failed or refused to fall back with the disintegrating remnants of their units. *Official USMC Photo*

Continued from page 92

artillery and naval gunfire weighed in with better results as soon as it became light. But the light played in both directions; it actually gave Japanese troops on dominating ground a better opportunity to hurt 3/21, which had held heroically through the night as Japanese advanced into the gap between it and the adjacent 9th Marines. After dawn, the 9th Marines had to withdraw along part of its front to man a counterattack to relieve 3/21. This attack was decisive, and the Japanese overlooking 3/21 were knocked from their perch. Throughout the morning, counterattacks in contested zones pushed the Japanese back from positions they had captured, but at great cost. Among those killed was the 2/3 commander. In the end, it took the commitment of an army battalion from the IIIAC reserve to man an effective sweeping force against the many

A psychological warfare team broadcasts an appeal for the beaten remnants of Guam's Japanese garrison to quit the fight while they can. Broadcasts were also made to Guam's Chamorro population, which was largely in hiding, that it was safe to cross into American lines. One surprise respondent was an American sailor who had been in hiding since the island was surrendered in December 1941. *Official USMC Photo*

As the battle wound down and the American advance reached toward every corner of the island, all hands were less and less willing to undertake unnecessary risks. The advances remained rapid because there were few Japanese to stand up to them, but they proceeded with great care and caution, and fighting was done at the longest possible range, where Japanese soldiers made a stand. *Official USMC Photos*

The American weapons in this cache will be put in the hands of armorers, who will rehabilitate them. The Japanese weapons will be studied for clues they might yield regarding the state of the Japanese industrial economy and then placed in storage or destroyed. *Official USMC Photo*

Japanese strongpoints intermingled with Marine positions. Long before the final Japanese infiltrators had been swept up or forced to retire, the decisive battle in the 3d Marine Division zone had been decided in favor of the Marines.

END GAME

There had never been a chance that Guam's defenders could prevail, but they might have delayed and thus weakened the American B-29 offensive for many weeks had they maintained a cohesive defensive effort in northern Guam. All chances for that were wiped away in their final counterattack on the night of July 25–26. The defense would remain stubborn, and the fall of northern Guam would not be completed until August 11, 1944, but that downfall was assured by Japanese actions on the night of July 25–26. Likewise, the Japanese defense of Orote Peninsula was stubborn and often brutal, but a foregone conclusion was reached on July 29 when the 4th and 22d Marines, attacking abreast, reached Orote Point.

Nearly 1,600 Marines died to capture Guam, as did 177 U.S. Army infantrymen, and 5,308 Marines and 662 GIs were wounded in action. At least eleven thousand Japanese soldiers and sailors died there, too.

Japanese dugouts, bunkers, pillboxes, and caves were blown up wherever they were found. If there were occupants who could be cajoled to surrender, they were spared and treated humanely. If they did not surrender, they were blown up where they hid. *Official USMC Photo*

This is what the road to Tokyo looked like. Large formations of veteran Marine infantrymen march on Guam's capital, Agana, as signalmen string phone lines alongside the highway. *Official USMC Photo*

A Tinian-based U.S. Army Air Forces B-24 heavy bomber on its return from a mission over the Bonin Islands. October 16, 1944. *Official USMC Photo*

4

UNSINKABLE AIRCRAFT CARRIERS

IN EACH CASE, AIRFIELDS ON SAIPAN, TINIAN, AND GUAM were rehabilitated as soon as engineers could safely get at them. The Saipan fields were initially employed by tactical fighters and light bombers that supported ground troops, at first on Saipan itself, then on Tinian and Guam. In short order, U.S. Army Air Forces bombers joined tactical aircraft on missions to nearby islands that were slated to be bypassed. Eventually, army air forces B-24 long-range heavy bombers arrived, and they visited Japanese holdings as far away as Iwo Jima, at first to reconnoiter such bases, and then to harass and bombard them. Meanwhile, as Tinian and Guam fell, work speeded up on the immense airfields the B-29s would need for their bombing campaign over Japan.

The first B-29s landed on Saipan on October 12, 1944, before even one airfield in the Marianas was completely ready to support B-29 combat operations. As the very heavy bomber force built up, training missions were run against bypassed island bases well within range, so airplanes, crews, tactics, and doctrine could be amply tested ahead of the real thing over heavily defended targets in Japan.

Several B-29 groups ran a training mission against Japanese-held Truk on October 28. On November 2, a Saipan-based B-29 photoreconnaissance variant became the first American airplane to fly over Tokyo since the April 1942 Doolittle raid. Six of seventeen B-29s dispatched from Guam attacked Iwo Jima on November 8 (at a range of nearly 650 miles), the first of several winter "training" missions to Iwo. Finally, on the night of November 24, 1944, 111 Marianas-based XXI Bomber Command B-29s were dispatched against targets in and around Tokyo. From that point, the Marianas-based B-29 campaign against Japan itself ramped up and became unremitting right to the last day of hostilities.

One of the new airfields on Saipan, filled to brimming with neat rows of tactical aircraft. *National Archives and Records Administration*

B-29s in one of the dispersal areas on a bomber base on Guam. *National Archives and Records Administration*

B-29s return from a mission. *National Archives and Records Administration*

Part II

PELELIU AND IWO JIMA

★ ★ ★ ★ ★

The invasion of Peleliu. *Official USMC Photo*

INTRODUCTION

OF THE THREE ISLAND INVASIONS left to the Marine Corps in mid-1944—before the anticipated invasion of Japan—Peleliu, Iwo Jima, and Okinawa—Peleliu turned out to be the least vital from a strategic perspective. It wasn't even technically within the Marine Corps' area of operations; it guarded the path from New Guinea, a U.S. Army objective, to the Philippines, another U.S. Army objective. But the twice-blooded 1st Marine Division was on hand to seize Peleliu, whose airfield was considered strategically vital when the plan was laid down. The Japanese knew this and they burrowed in deep to deflect what they read as a good situation for stalling or even deflecting the anticipated invasion of the southern Philippines.

The seizure of Iwo Jima, halfway between the Mariana Islands and Tokyo, was vital to the strategic bombing campaign that would precede and support the invasion of Japan. Moreover, Iwo Jima was the farthest southern outpost of the core Empire of Japan; it was home soil and thus well worth whatever assets needed to be deployed (and sacrificed) there to keep Japanese honor intact. In addition to filling the smallish island with as many ground troops as would fit, the Japanese planned to defend Iwo Jima with a giant naval force (that didn't exist anymore when the invasion took place) and a giant air-defense effort (that also never took place).

Marines advance on Iwo Jima.
Official USMC Photo

Marines assigned to seize Peleliu and Iwo Jima saw nothing but heavy fighting ahead.

Half of this part of *Islands of Hell* covers the bloody battle for Iwo Jima, whose photographic coverage was unparalleled elsewhere in the Pacific War in volume and sheer emotion. My 2006 book devoted to this battle, *Iwo Jima: Portrait of a Battle*, features 518 photos of the battle. There is no way to duplicate that exhaustive coverage here, in this much smaller space, but there was also no way to leave Iwo Jima out of this volume. I ended up with hundreds of unused Iwo Jima photos, which allowed me great latitude to select many photos that neither I nor any other author has previously consigned to print. Indeed, it is a conceit of this effort that I used the least number of previously published Iwo Jima photos possible while still providing a coherent photographic record of the brutal month-long bloodletting.

This montage of aerial photos shows Peleliu and surrounding islands. *National Archives and Records Administration*

5

PELELIU

★ ★ ★ ★ ★

September 15–October 15, 1944

WHY PELELIU?

AFTER THE FALL OF BUNA, NEW GUINEA, in January 1943, and of Guadalcanal in February, the course of the Pacific War seemed inevitable throughout the remainder of its days. Allied soldiers, sailors, and airmen pushed their way steadily along the Solomons chain and across the back of New Guinea for all of 1943, and the Americans began their long-awaited and always-preferred Central Pacific offensive at Tarawa and Makin in November 1943.

The logic that guided the advance from east to west and then south to north seemed to be firmly established as it unfolded. After securing eastern New Guinea (Papua), the Southwest Pacific Area forces under General Douglas MacArthur leapfrogged westward from base to base, often avoiding protracted and costly confrontations by landing where the Japanese had no strong fortifications. The same was true for the South Pacific Area forces under Vice Admiral William Halsey. A bypass strategy became firmly embedded in Allied policy wherever Japanese bases, both major and minor, could be evaded and contained. The bypass strategy became the favored outlook as the battle lines extended westward along New Guinea's endless-seeming northern coast and across the vast reaches of the Central Pacific. Tens and eventually hundreds of thousands of Japanese defenders on unwanted and unneeded bases were left, as Admiral Ernest King, the chief of naval operations, put it, "to wither on the vine." Of course, where conditions made it impossible to bypass a vitally needed but powerfully defended Japanese base, Allied commanders were in no way hesitant to overwhelm them by direct amphibious assault—as at Tarawa, Kwajalein, Eniwetok, Saipan, Tinian, and Guam. But many powerfully defended Japanese bases were bypassed or detoured, among them Rabaul, Truk, and numerous locations along the New Guinea coast.

By early August 1944, the twin Allied lines of advance seemed to be converging on the Philippine Islands. MacArthur's U.S. Sixth Army was in the Schouten Islands, off western New Guinea (Irian), and Admiral Chester Nimitz's advance across the vast Central Pacific had just about taken the Mariana Islands. Acting on the logic and reason that had thus far sustained the brilliantly successful (if often bloody) twin drives, the Central Pacific force would next turn north to jump into the Volcano Islands, a drive that would have taken these powerful amphibious and air forces directly toward Japan, and MacArthur's Southwest Pacific Area forces would have jumped into the southern Philippines, perhaps ending up in Formosa, or even the China coast between Hong Kong and Shanghai.

It was, in fact, the uncertainty of the ultimate goals and true direction of the next series of long reaches that were at the center of a major debate in the highest echelons of the

Three examples of pillboxes. The first is a rather elaborate and spacious emplacement constructed of coral blocks bonded with cement and covered with logs and loose coral blocks, the second is built from coral blocks and logs, and the third is a simple pit protected by log walls. *Official USMC Photos*

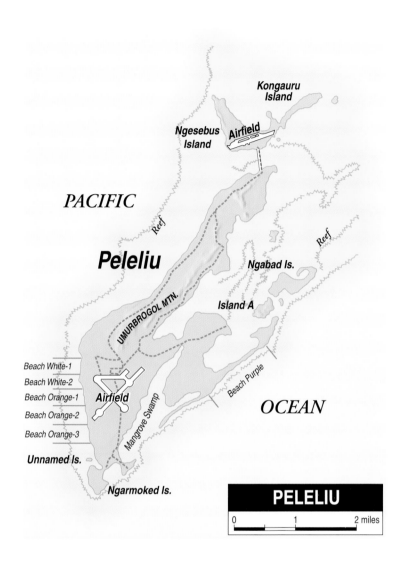

The rear entrance of this pillbox, which overlooks a likely landing beach, is built to keep out shrapnel and debris thrown up by a near miss. Note the level of overhead protection against a direct hit by a naval or artillery shell. Across the entire Pacific, the Japanese had proven themselves masters at building strong defenses from native materials. *Official USMC Photo*

American Pacific War leadership. Serious consideration was given to an invasion of Formosa and a landing at or near Amoy, China. The temptation to turn north from the Marianas toward Tokyo was tempered by a strategic view that pointed to the Volcano Islands as well as to Okinawa, through which an entry into the southernmost Japanese home island of Kyushu could be made, rather than a direct assault on Japan's centrally located capital.

Through the summer of 1944, as the Marianas invasion played itself out and as MacArthur's planners debated alternatives to a slow drive from south to north through the Philippines, a diversion of attention occurred. MacArthur's planners asked, quite rightly, how the Philippines invasion force was to be assured a safe passage from New Guinea to Mindanao if Japanese air bases in the Palau Islands were still in Japanese hands and intact. So far, none of the Caroline Islands—which stretch from Truk in the east to the Palaus in the west—had fallen into American hands. They had been bypassed for better invasion routes to the north and south, but there were still air routes in Japanese hands by which the bypassed (and only partially contained) Carolines bases could be sustained and reinforced. Only 500 air miles from the nearest Japanese air bases in the Philippines, the Palaus were particularly

Rear view of a 75mmn mountain gun set into the firing aperture of a coral-and-log emplacement overlooking some vital piece of terrain. Many such guns were set in for what amounted to ambush duty in a narrow defensive role, as opposed to providing general artillery coverage.
Official USMC Photo

This extremely elaborate position was to house a large-caliber naval gun that perhaps never reached Peleliu. Note that crew shelter and ammunition storage are provided within the concrete structure. *Official USMC Photo*

problematic in that they could be reached by air from the Japanese side without problem but were too far from the nearest American base to be powerfully and continuously interdicted from the air (a job for land-based bombers). It was true that the airfields in the Palaus had been raked clean by U.S. Navy carrier strikes on March 31, 1944, and it was further true that the many losses had not been replaced. Nevertheless, the Palaus air bases could be remanned and reinforced with great ease from the Philippines. If that happened, then the direct line of supply and communication running toward the Philippines from New Guinea could be attacked with great ease from them or from bases in the eastern Netherlands East Indies, especially in the Molucca Islands.

The reverse also was true. If Japanese land-based bombers could reach the Palaus from the Philippines, then Allied land-based bombers could reach the Philippines from the Palaus. Since the remote Palaus air bases could not be easily bombed into submission from any base in Allied hands at the time, and since Allied bombers based in the Palaus could help prepare the way for the inevitable Allied invasion of the Philippines, it seemed both necessary and useful that an invasion of the Palaus be mounted. (Most of the same holds true in the case of Japanese bases in the eastern Netherlands East Indies, and a parallel plan regarding the

A 5.5-inch dual-purpose naval gun has been set into a rudimentary emplacement on open ground. This versatile weapon, found on island bastions all across the Pacific, could be used for antiaircraft or antiboat defense, or as a general artillery piece, but it was especially vulnerable to preinvasion air attack and naval gunfire when emplaced in open antiaircraft positions like this. *Official USMC Photo*

Molucca Islands also was set in motion.) A look at a map makes a step to the Palaus appear as half a step backward from either the new Southwest Pacific Area bases in western New Guinea and the Schouten Islands, or a full step backward from the new Central Pacific bases in the Marianas. But given the ranges and positions of Allied and Japanese land-based bombers, half a step backward or a full step to the side into the Palaus appeared to be altogether necessary and perfectly logical by any measure available to the mid-1944 observer. The Allies knew this to be the case, and believed in it. So did the Japanese. Both sides prepared for an inevitable confrontation over the Palaus.

There were several possible objectives to consider for the projected Palaus invasion. The first, and seemingly the best, was

As the Pacific War progressed, the Japanese put more and more effort and assets into countering increasing numbers of American Sherman M4 medium tanks. The M4 was a mediocre tank in European combat, but it was usually the strongest weapon deployed in the Pacific. Shown here are a reasonably well-camouflaged antitank ditch and a 47mm antitank gun, either of which could disable an M4. *Official USMC Photos*

Of vital use to the Japanese on Peleliu, which had no ground water, was a system of concrete water-storage tanks. Many were breached in preinvasion attacks—deliberately to deny the defenders access to water, or because they looked like troop and weapons bunkers. Note the large hole blasted into the left side of this water tank. *Official USMC Photo*

This large, circular, steel-reinforced concrete bunker, which might have looked like a water tank from some angles, served as an Imperial Army sector command post. Note that three or four direct shell hits barely dented the structure. *Official USMC Photo*

the Japanese airfield complex on Babelthuap, by far the largest of the Palau islands. The second was a lesser air base on Peleliu, in the southern Palaus. And a third alternative was the seizure of an island that had no airfield but upon which a new bomber base could be built quickly. The third was actually the preferred scenario, and it was a proven method by that stage of the Pacific War, but alas, there was not enough time to create an invasion force, seize a suitable island, build a new base, and mount an aerial offensive against the Philippines in time to adequately precede the upcoming invasion of Mindanao. Intelligence in the form of Japanese documents captured on Saipan indicated that Babelthuap was very heavily defended, and it was too big to be taken quickly by any landing force of a size that could be harnessed in time. The airfield on Peleliu was smaller and less adequate than the one on Babelthuap, but it could be quickly expanded, and it seemed that it could be seized more easily by the two-division invasion force that could be made available. So, almost solely by a process of elimination, Peleliu was made the chief target of the largely preemptive Allied venture into the Palau Islands.

The Japanese had a special surprise planned for the veteran 1st Marine Division, to which the job of seizing Peleliu was given. Until that point in the war, Japanese defensive doctrine had favored a water's-edge defensive tactic coupled with ongoing massed-infantry attacks against the invading force. Almost without exception in the year-long trek across the Central Pacific, this ironclad rule had spelled doom for the defenders. If, as they always did, the invaders breached the water's-edge defenses, then the landing itself was secure. And if, as they always did, the main body of defenders threw themselves on the guns of the more numerous attackers, the defense degenerated into a series of isolated and incoherent actions against holed-up survivors.

Under a new formula issued by Imperial General Headquarters during the summer of 1944, the defenders of Peleliu and other potential invasion targets throughout Japan's shrinking Pacific empire were to hole up from the start and fight attritional battles throughout the length and breadth of their island bastions. Japanese ground troops who had done so on their own on Biak, in the Schouten Islands, had delayed an Allied victory far beyond the most pessimistic Allied estimate, and they had killed many more invasion troops than the island was worth.

Although the troops of the veteran and highly confident 1st Marine Division knew they would be facing more than ten thousand crack, battle-hardened Imperial Army troops on Peleliu, they had no idea that those Japanese would be dug in and prepared to defend themselves as no other Japanese ever faced by Marines in the Pacific.

D-DAY

Preceded by four days of very heavy bombardment by carrier aircraft and two days of very heavy bombardment by all manner of fire-support ships, the lead waves of the 1st Marine Division opened its assault on Peleliu's four southwestern invasion beaches at 0832 hours on September 15, 1944. (A simultaneous invasion was being launched by Southwest Pacific Area troops in the Molucca Islands.) The immediate objective of the Peleliu invasion was the southern fourth of the small island, for that is where the all-important airfield was located. Peleliu was to be a battle aimed at eradicating the foe, but getting Peleliu-based bombers into operation against targets in the Philippines was the prime strategic objective.

Landing on the division's left was the 1st Marine Regiment (1st Marines), whose lead waves made it to the beach without

As warships methodically pound targets ashore, carrier-based TBM light bombers pass overhead to bomb the island. *National Archives and Records Administration*

Peleliu's airfield is under air attack. The view is nearly due south, with landing beaches in view directly over the airfield. *Official USN Photo*

Marines go over the sides of their transport to take part in the 1st Marine Division's third island invasion, after Guadalcanal and Cape Gloucester. For the relative few who have weathered both earlier campaigns, Peleliu stands the chance of being the last Pacific battle before heading home. First, however, the Guadalcanal veterans must survive the battle before them, mostly as leaders of the rest in billets between regimental commander and fire-team leader. *Official USMC Photo*

Below: The lead waves of infantry and assault engineers will travel to the invasion beaches aboard amtracs from the III Amphibious Corps' (IIIAC's) 1st, 6th, and 8th Amphibian Tractor battalions, most of which are launched fully loaded from a flotilla of LSTs.
Official USMC Photos

much opposition but right away ran into formidable defenses on bluffs and other high ground to the immediate left. As more and more defenders recovered from the effects of last-minute bombardments or shifted toward the invaders from deep caves and shelters, the fire intensified against the leading troops as well as successive landing waves.

Charged with sealing a significant portion of the regiment's and the division's far-left flank, the 3d Battalion, 1st Marines (3/1) quickly counted itself lucky merely to have established a beachhead under such intense and dominating fire. Casualties ran very high. Indeed, Company K, 3/1, the division's left-flank unit, suffered grievous losses when it impaled itself on the heavily defended promontory upon which the division's left flank was to be anchored. Though Company K won a two-hour-long hand-to-hand struggle, the thirty-two survivors of its two-platoon assault force ended up being isolated from the rest of the division, unable to evacuate its casualties or receive supplies and replacements. To Company K's right, the remainder of 3/1 went to ground in swampy or open ground, and great unbridgeable gaps appeared. In sum, intense fire from hidden defenses caused 3/1 to end its first-day advance well short of nearly all its first-day objectives. On the regimental right, 2/1 ran into less opposition and thus was able to drive to the nearer of its two first-day objective lines. But 2/1's partial success caused it to lose contact with 3/1, so I/1 and

An LCI(R) rocket boat darts toward the beach, gunners firing 40mm guns at the smoke-shrouded shore as fellow crewmen prepare to fire clusters of rockets over the heads of the leading waves. Note the rocket racks along the side. *Official USMC Photo*

This still photo processed from motion-picture film appears to be the earliest view of Marines arriving ashore on Peleliu. The first troops ashore clocked in at 0832 hours. *Official USMC Photo*

Below: Marines under intense fire as soon as they left their amtracs sought whatever cover lay at hand. *Official USMC Photos*

numerous support troops had to be committed to cover the worst of the yawning gaps in the regimental line.

The 5th Marines had a somewhat easier time of it. Its drive across the island toward the southeastern shore was to take place across the open ground of the airfield, so its left flank was entirely exposed to fire from the heights and its advance was contested all along the front by dug-in Japanese. But the 5th Marines faced nothing like the intense near-in fire that had stalled the adjacent 1st Marines. On the regimental left, 1/5 reached its first phase line in good order, but it was obliged to hold there because 2/1, on its left, was held up. So 1/5 and several M4 medium tanks dug in to await developments on its flanks.

To the right of 1/5, 3/5's left company had no trouble landing or advancing, but the battalion's right company had trouble doing both, a situation that became worse when 3/7 landed on 3/5's beach because heavy defensive fires had forced it away from its own beach. Confusion slowed 3/5 at first, and then intense Japanese fire slowed the battalion, but its advance continued at a methodical pace against well-organized resistance that included accurate mortar barrages. At length, 2/5 had to be committed to bolster the advance, which was faltering due to battle and heat casualties. There also were problems maintaining contact with 3/7, on the right.

The 7th Marines landed across the southernmost beach in column of battalions—two battalions, actually, since 2/7 was the division reserve. Japanese fire forced most of 3/7 to land on the next beach to the north, behind 3/5, but the 7th Marines arrived ashore intact and not too badly hurt. There were confusion and

As they were able, with whatever means they could, the attackers dished it straight back into the defenders' faces. *Official USMC Photos*

Covered by an early-model armored amtrac, Marines and hospital corpsmen carry their wounded comrades to an ad hoc beachside aid station. *Official USMC Photo*

delays, but 3/7 sorted itself out and attacked toward the east. The job of the 7th Marines was to drive to the eastern shore and then wheel right to clear the southern portion of the island. Here, Marine tanks played a pivotal role in overcoming Japanese defensive emplacements and facilitating the advance. Terrain along 1/7's front was very swampy, so unit cohesion had to be sacrificed to keep the advance going. Opposition was based on numerous strongpoints, each of which had to be reduced as it was encountered. The truncated 7th Marines fought through the day, overcame many obstacles, and advanced deeply, but it reached none of its D-day objectives.

Although Peleliu's defenders had built a formidable defense-in-depth and were committed to a battle of attrition from which they frankly did not expect to escape, there was a counterattack plan. There was always some small hope that the landing force could be dislodged early in an amphibious assault, so a company of an estimated thirteen light tanks and an extremely well-trained infantry unit attacked behind an artillery and mortar preparation at nearly 1700 hours. The attack force surged across the open airfield,

continued on page 130

Marines advance inland where they can find or create chinks in the defenders' armor, but the tendency to bunch up and stall that has plagued every storm landing from Tarawa onward impinges the 1st Marine Division's striking power as more and more men and equipment pile up at and just inland from the surfline. It in no way helps the morale or confidence of men armored in dungaree shirts that the defenders do whatever they can—with great apparent success—to knock out amtracs and armored amtracs. *Official USMC Photos*

As the shock of first contact slowly wears off, the attackers go to work restoring unit integrity, moving up and down the beach to locate their comrades. In restoring unit integrity, Marines begin to fall back on the teamwork that has been at the heart of their training. *Official USMC Photo*

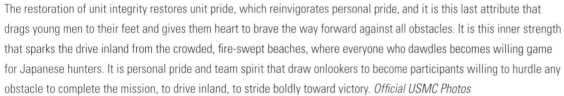

The restoration of unit integrity restores unit pride, which reinvigorates personal pride, and it is this last attribute that drags young men to their feet and gives them heart to brave the way forward against all obstacles. It is this inner strength that sparks the drive inland from the crowded, fire-swept beaches, where everyone who dawdles becomes willing game for Japanese hunters. It is personal pride and team spirit that draw onlookers to become participants willing to hurdle any obstacle to complete the mission, to drive inland, to stride boldly toward victory. *Official USMC Photos*

Long stretches of the invasion beaches are amply sown with mines, usually large antivehicle types that claim many amtracs and DUKW amphibian trucks. As soon as the infantry and its supports made room in the beachhead, engineers move in to locate, uncover, mark, and eventually disarm the deadly munitions. *Official USMC Photos*

The 1st Tank Battalion, which had been hovering off the reef in landing craft until called in, moved across the reef to the shore in the wake of the first inland assaults. *Official USMC Photo*

Command and control were restored and exerted as quickly as possible after the initial landings. The Marine with the handset is Lieutenant Colonel Austin Shofner, the commanding officer of 3/5. Shofner's was an amazing story: he had been captured by the Japanese on Corregidor, had escaped from his prisoner-of-war camp and fought beside Filipino and American guerrillas in the Philippines, had been evacuated from the Philippines by submarine, promoted to the rank of his contemporaries, and given command of a combat battalion on its way to battle. Unfortunately, this extremely aggressive battalion commander was wounded in a mortar barrage on D-day afternoon and not returned to duty until the Peleliu campaign was winding down. *Official USMC Photo*

Within a few hours of H-hour, the infantry regimental command posts had been established ashore and were working mightily to exert control on and provide services for a fiercely opposed inland drive. The consummate professionalism and unremitting drive of Marine senior commanders and their staffs at this stage of the war went a long, long way toward ensuring victory on increasingly bloody beaches. *Official USMC Photo*

Fearing the screw-ups and delays caused by reefs on earlier island battlefields, the 1st Pioneer Battalion's veteran commander had had several floating cranes built to expedite transshipment of ammunition and other supplies from deep-draft landing craft to amtracs and DUKWs. Landing craft could not get all the way to the beach, as the reef was too high or the lagoon was too shallow. The floating cranes evened out the flow all across the beachhead. *Official USMC Photo*

The first artillery ashore was a battery of 2/11's 75mm pack howitzers. Antitank obstacles on its designated beach obviated the use of amphibians to get the battery ashore, so the gunners manhandled the howitzers and all their ammunition and gear to a firing position right behind the 5th Marines. Other batteries that landed on D-day also walked ashore with their howitzers and gear. Shown here is the first Marine howitzer to fire on D-day, at 1605 hours. *Official USMC Photo*

This armored amtrac took out a Japanese 5.5-inch gun by the direct method because its gunner could not depress the main gun enough to fire at the target. The LVT(A) had to be towed out of the gun pit. *Official USMC Photo*

The main D-day assault petered out in midafternoon as the most advanced units reached open ground. Because adjacent units were held up and gaps might appear in the Marine front, these advanced units dug in at the verge of the airfield and along the edge of other defensible terrain. *Official USMC Photo*

The only organized Japanese counterattack of the Peleliu campaign jumped off at about 1700 hours on D-day. A well-trained infantry force that made good use of terrain during its approach attacked in a southwesterly direction across the broad expanse of the airfield in the company of an estimated thirteen light tanks, each armed with a 37mm main gun and one machine gun. The crews of Marine antitank weapons and M4 medium tanks, and even .30-caliber medium machine guns, coolly stood off to engage the attackers, most of whom were destroyed in the open. *Official USMC Photos*

Several Japanese light tanks—no one knows exactly how many—penetrated the Marine front line, and one or two nearly reached the beach. All of these tanks were destroyed when they were taken on by surprised but quick-acting rear-area troops, including the crew of a 75mm pack howitzer that blew its assailant to a halt with a direct hit by a high-explosives round, after which the stalled tank was destroyed by a bazooka gunner.
Official USMC Photo

Following an uncomfortable night of water shortages, minor probes, and a few concerted attacks, all three regimental combat teams moved out on D+1 to complete their D-day missions: the 1st Marines to gain a foothold in the ridge country north of the invasion beaches, the 5th Marines to capture the airfield and drive completely across Peleliu, and the two-battalion 7th Marines to drive across Peleliu and pivot southward to clear the southern tip of Peleliu. The 1st and 7th Marines fought hard but gained little traction; the 5th Marines completed its mission in day-long fighting. *Official USMC Photos*

Continued from page 122

diagonally across 2/1's front, and more or less directly toward 1/5, which had dug in earlier just off open ground precisely because it was known that Japanese tanks were part of the defensive team. Marine infantry weapons, 37mm antitank guns, and as many as a dozen M4 tanks intermingled with front-line infantry stood off and blasted the Japanese tanks and infantry, which were completely in the open. Several light tanks got into the Marine rear, where they were blown up by bazookas and direct artillery fire. Two tanks that became bogged down on swampy ground were abandoned, and two escaped. The attack force was crushed and, in its wake, elements of 2/5 were able to drive to the center of the airfield. Except for a few local forays, the attack was to be the only time the Japanese came out of their burrows to fight in the open. After this D-day attack, all the Japanese on Peleliu would have to be pried out of their fighting positions or blown up or incinerated in them.

By dusk, only two Marine companies had achieved their D-day goals. Though undermanned and isolated, Company K, 3/1, had anchored the division's left, and Company L, 3/5, had completely crossed the island to the eastern shore. Otherwise, eight Marine infantry battalion landing teams were strewn across the length and breadth of the southern fourth of Peleliu. Heavy counterattacks were expected during the night. There was plenty of night action, but no big attack materialized, which in a way was disappointing because the invasion plan counted on the suicidal tactics Marines had overcome all along the way from Tarawa to Guam.

Marine casualties on D-day were heavy: 210 dead and 901 wounded, not including hundreds of heat cases caused by scorching daytime temperatures coupled with inadequate water supplies. There was concern that casualties were so high and that so few objectives had been seized, but everyone was fundamentally optimistic that D+1 would be a much better day, for the 1st Marine Division was firmly established on Peleliu and in possession of enormous offensive strength relative to the living defenders.

THE AIRFIELD AND SOUTHERN PELELIU

On D+1, Marine medium tanks came into their own, as they never had to this point in the Pacific War. The grinding advance across Peleliu probably could not have taken place as well as it did without the incredible bravery and selfless devotion exhibited by the 1st Tank Battalion's M4 crews. They were magnificent. Often as not, despite heavy small-arms fire at every point, tank commanders stood upright in open hatches to see targets in Peleliu's jumbled,

closed terrain. Casualties among the tank commanders were very high. Most, perhaps all, of the battalion's medium tanks were knocked out at one time or another during the campaign, but most were speedily returned to duty by expert, dedicated repair crews. The tanks made all the difference on Peleliu.

The infantry was no less magnificent. It took utmost teamwork and bravery to advance on hidden, mutually supporting bunkers and caves, and these were traits the Marine infantry possessed in abundance. With or without the support of the tanks, the infantry steadily reduced bunker after bunker, cave after cave, defensive locale after defensive locale. The price was exorbitant, but the gains from D+1 onward were often considerable.

On D+1, the two-battalion 7th Marines advanced to the eastern shore in its zone and then wheeled smartly to the south to take on the defenses between the airfield and the southern point of the island. Both battalions of the 7th Marines had to halt in place at one time or another to await the arrival of fresh water. The heat caused as many casualties as enemy fire, and would do so throughout the battle. Most of the 7th Marines' objectives were taken on D+1, but the truncated regiment was unable to take the last of its southern objectives until D+3, September 18. In accomplishing its mission, the regiment destroyed a reinforced battalion of Japanese infantry amounting to 2,609 known enemy dead, about a fourth of the

continued on page 137

This sniper was flushed out well to the rear of the 5th Marines' front line. Quite a number of Marines were taken from their formal duties to provide security in the crowded rear areas, which slowed both the expansion and the efficient organization of the beachhead. *Official USMC Photo*

Starting at dawn, the 5th Marines crashed into the airfield, which incorporated the island administrative center and numerous machine and maintenance shops, warehouses, and living quarters that had to be reduced building by building. The early and aggressive commitment of tanks and antitank weapons provided plenty of punch in support of the maneuvering infantry.
Official USMC Photos

Throughout the early days of the campaign, boarding parties built around armored amtracs combed the shore and numerous seemingly abandoned Japanese landing craft and other vessels for snipers whose work hampered the buildup of supplies and equipment in the beachhead. The mission shown in this photo led to the deaths of one Japanese officer and six enlisted men and the capture of one enlisted man. *Official USMC Photo*

Despite the commitment of three amtrac battalions and several DUKW companies, the landing and buildup phases were severely hampered by an ongoing shortage of amphibian trucks and tractors. An LST, seen here retrieving a damaged LVT(A), was set aside for amtrac and DUKW repairs, but mine damage and losses to grinding overwork overwhelmed this effort at the outset, and soon numerous damaged amphibians were sidelined for as long as a few days while awaiting repairs. By this phase of the island-hopping campaign, amtracs and DUKWs bore the brunt of transport duties from reef to shore and then inland over broken ground to front-line units. The mere delay of just drinking water to the front line caused by sidelined amtracs led to an alarming rise in heat casualties, which weakened the offensive by sidelining the heat cases themselves as well as the many more Marines and corpsmen needed to get them safely to aid stations. Ammunition was in short supply at the front for the same reason, and that also slowed the offensive to gain more ground for the establishment of secure dumps that much closer to the front, which further stressed the amphibians. *Official USMC Photo*

Lack of water caused casualties; the precipitous rise in heat casualties weakened combat units; and weaker combat units had more trouble overcoming their objectives, which led to a higher rate of battle casualties. Three medical-surgical companies of the 1st Medical Battalion were sent ashore very early in the battle, but lack of transport kept their equipment and supplies from being landed until September 21. Though the shortage of transport into the beach was bordering on the disastrous, LVTs and DUKWs heading back to the transport fleet were up to the job of carrying casualties to the many transports and LSTs with medical facilities aboard. For all that, hard fighting under unbearable human conditions led to an alarming rate of deaths in a battle that was supposed to have been "routine" for that stage of the war.
Official USMC Photos

All four battalions of the 11th Marines, less two 105mm howitzers sunk aboard DUKWs, were ashore on September 16, and at least a battalion was always on call by each infantry regiment on Peleliu. *Official USMC Photos*

Once the artillery and some carrier-based air support had done what it could to soften targets ahead of the battle line, it was up to infantrymen working alongside halftracks and tanks to advance and reduce the well-hidden pillboxes and bunkers that honeycombed the 7th Marines' sector in southern Peleliu. *Official USMC Photos*

Continued from page 131

original defenders. The cost, overall, was 47 killed, 37 missing in action, and 414 wounded.

The 5th Marines and 2/1 succeeded in driving across the entire airfield complex, reaching the eastern shore, and sealing the southern portion of the island from infiltration from the northeast. The division reserve, 2/7, was landed on D+1, attached to the 1st Marines, and used to bridge a widening gap between the stalled 1/1 and the advancing 2/1. By day's end on September 16, a continuous if extremely jagged line ran across the entire island somewhat to the north of the airfield and, on the left and in the center, somewhat into the southern verge of Peleliu's central ridge complex, upon which the bulk of the diehard Japanese would be basing their stand.

THE PENINSULA

On D+3, after containing the Japanese defensive zone in the southeastern ridge area north of the airfield, the reinforced 5th Marines (less 1/5, in division reserve) attacked into a rather large

The 5th Marines stormed into Peleliu's so-called Peninsula with all the combat savvy its troops had picked up in two earlier campaigns, Guadalcanal and Cape Gloucester. The eastern region of Peleliu was lightly defended compared to the Umurbrogol Mountains to the west, and the flat terrain aided the attackers, but it was tough going as long as the Japanese resisted. *Official USMC Photos*

Efforts were made from early in the battle to talk defenders out of their burrows via portable loudspeaker systems, but there were very few takers on Peleliu. Of those who did surrender, most were Korean slave laborers. *Official USMC Photo*

This flamethrower amtrac is a homegrown product of local ingenuity; the system is not known to have been used on other island battlefields. The flamethrower itself is the large version usually deployed in flame tanks. *Official USMC Photo*

but isolated eastern extension of Peleliu, almost a separate island adjacent to the main island, known as the Peninsula. Here, and on several small, adjacent islands in the regimental sector, hundreds of Japanese defenders were killed in their burrows between September 18 and September 23, when the Peninsula was ultimately declared secure.

BATTLE FOR THE RIDGES

In stark contrast to the bloody but successful drives by the 5th and 7th Marines in their zones, the 1st Marines (including 2/7 from D+2) was extremely hard-pressed as it advanced into the well-defended ridge country north of the airfield—the so-called Umurbrogol Mountains. Western Peleliu is actually centered on a ridge of coral that was driven up from the sea bottom by an earthquake in the distant past. Thus the central ridge is little more than a shattered coral reef thrown into the air. The Japanese had spent months feverishly improving

This aerial photo amply illustrates the requirement that dominating high ground be taken completely into Marine hands. The feature here is Bloody Nose Ridge, the objective of the reinforced 1st Marines beginning on D+1. *Official USMC Photo*

Another aerial view of Bloody Nose Ridge taken from over the western shore. The main battle for the Umurbrogol Mountains took place between the parallel roads seen at top and bottom of this view. *Official USMC Photo*

Sheer walls and broken ground down to sea level characterized most of the terrain in the Umurbrogols. *Official USMC Photo*

on nature's handiwork, and the result—nature's and the defenders'—was simply awesome, all but impenetrable. Tanks were helpful on the verges, where they could find suitable ground, but they could not get up to the central areas once Marine infantrymen passed beyond range or line of sight. Artillery and air support were ample, but both were largely ineffective against deep caves. Because the artillery was free to fire at any time, the airplanes could not get low enough against hillsides facing the advance to hit individual caves and burrows with any degree of accuracy. And the artillery could not reach the many Japanese hiding holes on the reverse slopes of the craggy, broken coral Umurbrogol Mountains. For the most part, then, artillery fired over the heads of Marines in the assault, and air endeavored to hit the defilade slopes.

Throughout D+1—September 16—3/1 and 1/1 attempted to attack into the first line of ridges north of the open airfield area, a feature Marines dubbed Bloody Nose Ridge, but both battalions were stymied by heavy fire from large numbers of defensive emplacements dug into unbelievably broken terrain. By D+3 the four battalion landing teams assigned to the 1st Marines had bogged down entirely in the center and then had to halt on the left on

Every troop movement seemed to be against gravity. *Official USMC Photo*

The Umurbrogol ridges, composed of coral, were honeycombed with natural caves made formidable by Japanese ingenuity. Here, the Marine at left center is caught in the act of hurling a grenade at the mouth of a cave he and his comrades stumbled on while trailing another Marine unit. The Japanese often undertook "passive infiltration," which only involved lying silent as front-line Marine units passed by their burrows, then attacking rear echelons. It took an awful lot of combat troops to systematically comb and recomb supposedly secure ground to neutralize these stay-behinds, and even then the Japanese often evaded such dragnets. *Official USMC Photo*

Long after the 1st Marines had pushed well north along Bloody Nose Ridge, a covey of Japanese snipers plied its trade along the supposedly pacified beach drive, West Road. The embattled 1st Marines had not the troops to comb the area, and neither did the 1st Marine Division. The sign just south of Dead Man's Curve reads: "Danger. Sniper fire along road next mile. Keep moving. No parking on road." As late as October 3, Colonel Joseph Hankins, the division headquarters commandant, was shot in the head and killed by one of these snipers. *Official USMC Photo*

Tanks, which were at the heart of Marine Corps assault doctrine by this phase of the war, were only marginally useful at the verges of the twisted ridge country. This blade tank fires its 75mm main gun pointblank into a Japanese-held cave as infantrymen guide the gunner onto the target. *Official USMC Photo*

D+5 to remain in possession of a coherent line. The regiment fought bravely—perhaps too bravely, for it shattered itself in eking out gains that ultimately were too small to justify the loss of so many magnificent troops. In the first three days on Peleliu, the reinforced 1st Marines sustained 1,236 battle casualties, nearly a third its original strength. By D+5, more than 1,500 members of the regiment had been killed or wounded, and this does not take into account a steady, debilitating stream of heat casualties.

On September 20, three of the 1st Marines' four infantry battalions were relieved by 1/7 and 3/7. Gallant attacks into the

continued on page 146

A flamethrower amtrac cooks a cave high up on a steep slope. *Official USMC Photo*

The 1st Marine Division's 11th Marines landed three 105mm howitzer battalions and one 75mm pack howitzer battalion, an artillery force made formidable by the addition of IIIAC's two 155mm howitzer battalions. But the artillery was positioned south of the Umurbrogols and thus could fire only at southward-facing terrain features. Seen here is a 155mm howitzer. *Official USMC Photo*

Artillery and some air support—and even some infantry maneuvers—were guided by observers aboard Marine Corps light observation aircraft, a variety of makes and models that were all dubbed OY. The 1st Marine Division's observation squadron, VMO-3, mounted its first missions from a corner of Peleliu airfield on D+3, after flying ashore from an escort carrier. *Official USMC Photo*

By late 1944, only Marine artillery regiments still had 75mm artillery weapons in their inventories. This photo illustrates why. In its capacity as an expeditionary organization, the Marine Corps clung to the doctrine that a Marine division ought to be self-contained and on-call with an ability to meet any of its own needs. The 105mm and 155mm howitzers available on Peleliu had to be deployed on solid, flat terrain in southern Peleliu, but 2/11's much lighter 75mm pack howitzers, which could be broken down into four man-packable main components, could be moved to high ground via steep slopes with just ropes, pulleys, and muscle power. This pack howitzer is being levitated to high ground to help infantrymen conquer a feature known as Death Valley. *Official USMC Photo*

If they benefited from any vista at all in the tortured and overgrown coral ridges, .30-caliber machine guns employed in the Umurbrogols typically provided suppressive fire and overwatch protection for infantry teams moving in on suspected Japanese positions. *Official USMC Photo*

This 60mm mortar crew has set up the weapon without its baseplate, which was no doubt jettisoned to save weight in the hilly terrain. Note the aiming stake at top center.
Official USMC Photo

In the near absence of traditional stand-off support weapons, some of the best direct-fire support the Marines had at hand in the ridge battles was the relatively new 2.36-inch (60mm) rocket launcher dubbed bazooka. The shape-charge warhead, designed to penetrate a tank hull, could damage or destroy many caves and dugouts. The downside was that a bazooka gave away its position when the backblast from the departing rocket kicked up a huge cloud of dust and debris. Presumably this bazooka gunner is wearing his gas mask as an antidote to getting debris in his eyes. *Official USMC Photo*

Rarely used by Marines in World War II, the rifle grenade came into its own in Peleliu's ridge country, where opposing forces often hunkered down on opposite sides of the same ridge. The grenade fired from the M1 rifle was a modified "pineapple" fragmentation hand grenade affixed to a special launcher assembly. This photo, and the next two, were taken during a small-unit clash on Suicide Hill. *Official USMC Photo*

Continued from page 143

teeth of Japanese-held defensive complexes continued for three more days, to little avail. Only then did Marine commanders conclude that the strategically vital portions of the island—the airfield, and little else—had been in their hands for nearly a week.

By September 22, the bulk of the U.S. Army's green but well-trained 81st Infantry Division had seized most of neighboring Angaur Island and thus was available to relieve elements of the 1st Marine Division on Peleliu. This was done in days. (The 81st Division's third regimental combat team almost bloodlessly seized Ulithi Atoll between September 21 and 23. Ulithi was turned into the Pacific Fleet's westernmost anchorage and base for the remainder of the war.)

The decision to contain the Umurbrogols and turn the island over to the 81st Infantry Division took virtually all the pressure off the battered 1st Marine Division. Army troops began to replace the Marines around the Umurbrogol Pocket on September 23.

Easy pickings to the north still remained to be harvested. The battered, fought-out 1st Marines replaced the 5th Marines

In this photo of the same action (the grenadier is at far left), several Molotov cocktails have been ignited, and one is about to be tossed over the ridgeline. The burning fuel can engulf an emplacement or cave, or it can flush men hiding in the brush by setting the vegetation afire. *Official USMC Photo*

The Japanese hardly sat and took the deadly shower of grenades and flames. In this final photo in the series, one of the Marines has been wounded, perhaps while peering over the ridgeline, and his buddies are helping him to the ground so they can begin to render first aid. *Official USMC Photo*

The battlefield in the Umurbrogols was 360 degrees all the time.
Official USMC Photo

as the Peninsula's garrison; then the 5th Marines was carried by trucks around the western side of the Umurbrogol Pocket to mount a lightly contested grab of northern Peleliu that culminated in an amphibious landing on neighboring Ngesebus Island. These moves contained the Umurbrogol Mountains from virtually all quarters and left the conduct of air operations from the rehabilitated airfield in virtual peace. Organized Japanese resistance ceased in northern Peleliu on September 30, after which an army regimental combat team relieved the 5th Marines north of the Umurbrogols.

By October 7, the 7th Marines had been so weakened by sustained combat that it had to be replaced on the line by the moderately rested 5th Marines. Marine infantry battalions rotated

continued on page 152

Scenes from a Battlefield

Official USMC Photos

Corpsmen work feverishly to save this wounded Marine, but the young man succumbed to his wounds. *Official USMC Photo*

There is always someone who will show the way forward. *Official USMC Photo*

Twelve Japanese soldiers were killed when a tank fired its 75mm main gun directly into their cave, followed by flames from a flamethrower. *Official USMC Photo*

Continued from page 148

into and out of combat assignments until October 12, when the "assault" phase was declared at an end. On October 15, the 1st Marine Division was formally relieved of its combat role in the Palaus, and large elements of the division began to leave Peleliu on October 30. It was not until November 27, however, that the Umurbrogol Pocket was eradicated by army troops and the island declared secure.

A total of 6,265 Marines became casualties on Peleliu—1,124 killed, 117 missing, and 5,024 wounded or injured. It is estimated that 10,695 Japanese died on Peleliu, and 301 were taken prisoner.

This is one of the last photos taken of Marines in ground action on Peleliu. *Official USMC Photo*

AIR POWER

Development of the airfield—Peleliu's strategic prize—began as soon as the complex fell into Marine hands on D+2. A U.S. Navy TBM carrier bomber was the first American airplane to land there, on September 18, and two VMO-3 OY artillery spotter planes arrived for permanent duty on the same day. An advance flight echelon of Marine Air Group 11's VMF(N)-541 arrived on September 24, VMF-114 arrived on September 26, and VMF-122 and the rest of VMF(N)-541 arrived on October 1. All of these Marine aircraft (and others that followed) were deployed at Peleliu to fulfill a tactical role—to support the ground troops—or to interdict bypassed Japanese bases in the western Carolines that were within their range.

The *strategic* purpose for attacking the Palau Islands was to put the newly captured and expanded airfield at the disposal of long-range bombers that could mount preinvasion attacks against Japanese bases in the southern Philippines. This mission was never accomplished. In the first place, a decision made on September 15—the very day the 1st Marine Division invaded Peleliu—moved the initial invasion target in the Philippines from Mindanao, in the south, to Leyte, in the center. Moreover, the date of the U.S. return to the Philippines was advanced from December 20, 1944, to October 20. The first Peleliu-based U.S. Army Air Forces preinvasion heavy-bomber mission to the Philippines took place on October 17, and the invasion of Leyte took place on October 20. At most, a few tens of tons of bombs were

As soon as Marine Corps F4U Corsair fighter-bombers were based at Peleliu, most were used to drop napalm on hard-to-reach Japanese-held features in the Umurbrogols. The main threat to the pilots, who faced very little hostile fire, was from Marine artillery, which had no restrictions on where or when it fired in response to urgent calls from the infantry. Seen here, groundcrewmen fix an empty napalm tank to the Corsair's center-line bomb shackle; the tank will be filled with the napalm mixture and fitted with an igniter shortly before taking off. *Official USMC Photo*

Coming in low, this Corsair's pilot releases the napalm tank over Five Sisters Ridge early enough for momentum to drag it just over the ridgeline, where smoke from an earlier napalm drop is spreading. Each Corsair circles back to the airfield to rearm for another go. *Official USMC Photos*

delivered from Peleliu before the Philippines invasion began. On October 21, the built-from-scratch runway on Angaur—an island taken at very little cost—was declared operational, and heavy-bomber operations from there commenced within days.

SUMMING UP

The bold facts, seen so clearly in hindsight, are that Peleliu need not have been invaded—that Angaur alone (if any Palaus objective at all) would have sufficed, and at much reduced cost in blood. This detracts nothing whatever from the utmost bravery and sacrifice exhibited and endured by the superb 1st Marine Division between September 15 and October 15, 1944. As in the case of Cape Gloucester, also taken by the 1st Marine Division, the seizure of Peleliu seemed necessary and vital while it was happening. It is ironic and extremely sad that, like Cape Gloucester, Peleliu turned out to be worth almost none of the lives and limbs expended there. But thousands of brave 1st Division Marines once again did their duty at Peleliu, and nothing can ever detract from that.

Official USMC Photo

An aerial photo of Iwo Jima, taken from west to east, shows two completed airfields (right and left center of the island) and the uncompleted third airfield (far left center). Mount Suribachi is at the far right (southern) tip of the island. *National Archives and Records Administration*

6

IWO JIMA

★ ★ ★ ★ ★

February 19–March 16, 1945

WHY IWO JIMA?

IWO JIMA—SULFUR ISLAND—IS ONE OF THE MOST ISOLATED places on Earth. Waterless and barren, it is unsubtly hostile to human settlement. Nevertheless, as in days predating the opening of Japan to the world in the mid-nineteenth century, Iwo Jima rests at the very outer limit of the Empire of Japan. Its only economic function has been the export of sulfur, a by-product of the volcanic action that seethes barely beneath the island's mantle.

During the Pacific War, once its small civilian populace was evacuated, Iwo Jima had only two functions: as a watchpost against invasion of the inner empire, and as the seat of an air base complex built to enhance its garrison's watch mission. But its importance to Japan in late 1944 and early 1945 was also emotional: Iwo Jima was true Japanese soil, an integral component of the empire. Also, because it could support several large airfields—which nearby islands could not—it would naturally come under the eye of the American naval, air, and amphibious forces sweeping across the vast Pacific toward the Japanese home islands. The reasons for stoutly defending the otherwise useless and barren volcanic speck was first one of honor, for Iwo Jima was intrinsically Japanese; second was to deny the Americans the airfield sites for as long as possible; and third, to lay down the gauntlet, to communicate to the onrushing Americans that all of Japan would be as stoutly, as heroically, as unremittingly defended as was tiny, useless—but oh, so Japanese—Iwo.

The bloodbath at Iwo Jima in February and March 1945 owes itself entirely to the exigencies of the air war in the Pacific as a whole and specifically to the needs of the culminating phase of the strategic air offensive against the Japanese home islands.

Until mid-1944, when U.S. Marine and army divisions seized Japanese-held Saipan, Tinian, and Guam in the Mariana Islands, the Allied Pacific War strategy had been hobbled by the operational range (i.e., the effective combat radius) of land-based fighters. Simply

No decision had been made regarding an invasion site in the Volcano or neighboring Bonin islands when bases there were attacked for the first time in early July 1944 by two carrier groups (eight aircraft carriers) and surface warships. Shown here is a pilot's eye view of a July 4 bombing mission against the harbor at Chichi Jima, the most developed military base in the area and, for a time, the leading candidate for invasion. At this stage of the war, Iwo Jima fielded a reasonably robust air contingent and a small ground garrison. The air contingent was swept from the skies by American carrier fighters, and the ground garrison was pummeled to dust by American warships that fired from close in without fear of island-based guns. Indeed, it was this alarming demonstration of vulnerability that started the wheels turning to create the fortress that challenged the ingenuity and survival skills of U.S. Marines seven months later. *Official USN Photo*

Essex-class fleet aircraft carriers were the backbone of the U.S. Navy striking power from late 1943 onward. It was carrier air, more than powerful surface gunnery platforms, that made the island-hopping campaign as robust and flexible as it turned out to be, for carrier battle groups, each centered on up to four fleet and light carriers, could go anywhere—strike anywhere—they were needed, either in direct support of an island invasion or to pummel Japanese bases far from the scene of current land action. Indeed, once the fast carrier task force grew to four carrier task groups fielding a total of up to sixteen fleet and light carriers, one, two, or three task groups could support ground operations while the remaining task groups simultaneously struck one or even two distant targets. *Official USN Photo*

An important innovation that gave the fast carrier task force its immense flexibility, beginning in late 1943, was the all-out development of a fleet of, by war's end, more than a hundred escort carriers (CVEs), such as the one shown here. In the Pacific, the "jeep" carriers might simply transport airplanes across vast distances, or they might accompany the fast carriers to supply replacement airplanes and pilots to make good combat or operational losses. But from Tarawa onward, they were used increasingly during island invasions as floating bases for dedicated ground-support fighters and light bombers. It was this last use that gave the fast carrier task force its immense operational flexibility, for the big carriers did not have to be tethered to a fixed position to provide ongoing, long-term invasion support because the ground-support CVEs were more than up for the job and, indeed, the airmen who flew from them were specially trained and armed to undertake direct support of ground troops. *Official USN Photo*

put, to run an effective land-based bombing campaign against Japanese-held Pacific island bases, the U.S. Army Air Forces and Marine air commands in the Pacific had to provide numerous and effective fighter escorts. So, though bombers outranged fighters by a considerable margin, the advance up the Solomons chain in 1942 and 1943, along the northern coast of New Guinea from late 1942 to mid-1944, across the central Pacific in late 1943 through mid-1944, and through the Philippines from October 1944, had to take place at a pace of up to 300 miles per hop if the objective was to seize airfield sites from which Japanese bases farther out could be interdicted by fighter-escorted land-based bombers.

This linkage between the Allied Pacific offensive and the operational range of fighters (which was less than half their actual range) held up as a military law of nature until the unveiling of the U.S. Navy's fast carrier task force in November 1943. At that point, as new fleet carriers and light carriers began to arrive in the Pacific war zone at an average rate of more than one per month, the 300-mile law could be bent somewhat if enough carriers could be shackled to a new objective long enough for ground troops to either seize an existing airfield that could be *quickly* rehabilitated, or to clear room for the *rapid* installation of a new airfield. As land-based fighters and fighter-bombers moved up to the new airfield,

Dispatching groups of fast carriers deep into enemy territory was fraught with serious risk of loss of one or more carriers and thousands of lives—a real threat that could lengthen the war and cause countless ripple effects even though the ultimate outcome was not the least bit in doubt. Though the American submarine fleet had nearly choked off all supplies entering or leaving Japan by sea, the ultimate battle foreseen by Allied planners was to be in the Japanese home islands following mass invasion by ground forces. Though the fast carrier force was to exceed forty flight decks by mid-1945, this was in no way sufficient to throttle Japanese industry prior to an October 1945 invasion. By mid- and late 1944, only long-range heavy bombers could even begin to do that job, and the only candidate was the very-long-range B-29 very-heavy bomber, whose deployment and use guided the island-hopping campaign from the June 1944 invasion of the Marianas to the decision to wrest Iwo Jima from Japanese control during the first quarter of 1945. Seen here is a flight of B-29s based in the Mariana Islands. *Official USAAF Photo*

land-based bombers also could be brought forward, to support invasion troops ashore as well as to strike nearby bases that had been kept under the gun to that point by carrier air. At that point, the full weight of the fast carrier task force could be used to soften up new targets beyond the range of land-based fighters and, as the central Pacific campaign progressed, even beyond the range of land-based bombers. The addition of numerous escort carriers to the invasion fleets from late 1943 substantially enhanced the reach of the fast carriers, because escort-based air squadrons were trained and equipped to guard the invasion fleet *and* provide air support for forces ashore. Thus more fast carriers could move on to more distant assignments sooner than had been the case prior to the organization of flotillas of escort carriers.

The technological leap that nearly severed the link between the length of a new step forward and the operational range of land-based fighters was the appearance of U.S. Army Air Forces Boeing B-29 Superfortress very heavy bombers. These aerial giants, which were first employed out of forward bases in China, were built to fly at 32,000 feet—higher than most Japanese defensive fighters could reach—as well as to carry four tons of bombs out to ranges of 1,600 miles, and return. This was about 5,000 feet higher and 600 miles farther *in each direction* than the Consolidated B-24 Liberator heavy bomber.

The seizure of Saipan, Tinian, and Guam placed nearly all of Japan within range of a B-29-based bombing offensive as soon as highly reinforced, extra-long runways could be built on the three

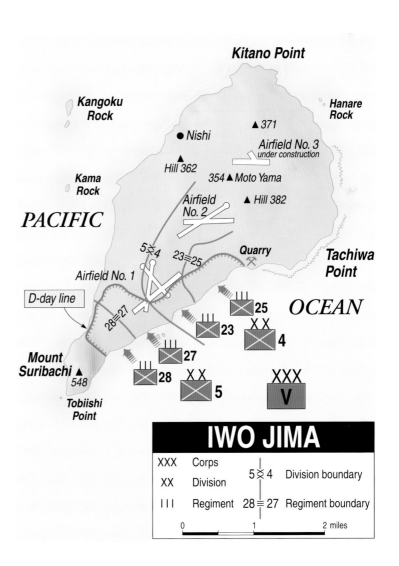

islands. The first B-29s reached Saipan on October 12, 1944; several groups ran a training mission against Japanese-held Truk on October 28; and six of seventeen B-29s dispatched from Guam attacked Iwo Jima on November 8 (at a range of nearly 650 miles), the first of several winter "training" missions to Iwo. Finally, on the night of November 24, 1944, 111 Marianas-based XXI Bomber Command B-29s were dispatched against an aircraft factory in Tokyo. Just one of these B-29s was lost, when rammed by a Japanese fighter.

Other than as a practice target for newly arrived B-29 groups, Iwo Jima as yet had no direct role in the B-29 strategy, but it stood at the apex of a shallow equilateral triangle roughly half the distance between the Marianas and central Japan.

By early 1945, all three of the U.S. Army Air Forces' long-range, high-altitude fighter types of the day—Lockheed P-38 Lightnings, Consolidated P-47 Thunderbolts, and North American P-51 Mustangs—had been refined to the point at which their operational range was more than the distance between Iwo Jima and Tokyo. In other words, Iwo Jima, as an air base, stood at an optimum point for emergency landings by damaged or malfunctioning B-29s on their way to or from Japan and the Marianas—*and* as the extreme launch point for long-range fighters that could provide day escort for B-29s over Japanese cities and industrial zones.

In a nutshell, Iwo Jima or a neighboring island in the Volcano or Bonin island groups were the most suitable sites for both an emergency airfield and advance fighter base in support of the upcoming strategic bombing offensive against the Japanese homeland. All of the calculus by which invasion targets were selected that late in the Pacific War ground out inexorable results to all of the mathematical inputs bound up in distances and even in the tradeoffs in lives laid on the line to seize the bases, as opposed to lives saved by having airfields available for emergency landings, not to mention fighter escorts that could reach central Japan. Indeed, twin-engine North American B-25 medium bombers (designated PBJ by the Marine Corps) would be able to attack Japanese shipping and shore targets in southern Japan from Iwo Jima, a minor but nonetheless interesting bonus.

This is one of scores of 5-inch naval-type antiaircraft/antiboat guns set in all across Iwo Jima by its defenders. This example is set into a well-built, well-sited antiaircraft emplacement with a good view of the invasion beaches, but many others were set into elaborate, highly resistant steel-reinforced concrete bunkers. *Official USMC Photo*

A very large part of the defensive system that honeycombed all of Iwo Jima was based on groups of natural caves that were strongly enhanced by the garrison as it grew from a few hundred in mid-1944 to about 23,000 by mid-February 1945. *Official USMC Photo*

Seen here is an example of the many elaborate and extremely well-built concrete-and-steel bunkers that virtually carpeted the island. This is a multi-level system with a pillbox-type gun emplacement on top and a sheltering stone-reinforced trench running around the base. Note the use of earth to camouflage the bunker against aerial observation as well as to deflect the killing power of bombs and naval shells. *Official USMC Photo*

All of about two dozen Japanese light tanks that reached Iwo Jima were dug in and thus immobilized. They served as steel pillboxes until destroyed, usually by direct attack. *Official USMC Photo*

Here is a short section of the 11 miles of caves that were constructed beneath Iwo's surface at depths to 75 feet. This cave, which is lined with uniform blocks of local basaltic rock, is topped off with logs upon which an earthen roof has been placed. It is probably a fairly shallow system, but it certainly survived intact if any large-caliber shells struck the overhead. *Official USMC Photo*

There were other islands in the vicinity of Iwo Jima that would have been fine as advance support bases that late in the war, but Iwo Jima was the only one that had the topography that could support the very long runways required by the B-29s. The Japanese did not realize this, because they knew very little about the B-29 program. Nevertheless, they very well comprehended the offensive value Iwo Jima would have if the largest, longest-ranged American heavy bomber of the last phase of the Pacific War would have remained the B-24, because B-24s based at or staging through Iwo Jima from the Marianas would nonetheless have access to nearly all of Japan. Moreover, they knew that Iwo-based, state-of-the-art fighter escorts would be able to range over all of the southern two-thirds of Japan.

Even without factoring in the B-29 program, the Japanese knew that Iwo Jima was a highly likely target of American strategic planners, so they decided to defend it as heavily as their reeling war industry and burgeoning manpower needs could support. The fact that Iwo Jima stood at the extremity of the prewar Japanese Empire added honor—and thus intractable stubbornness—to the mix of defensive priorities in a way American invasion forces had not yet experienced in the Pacific.

FORTRESS IWO

Iwo Jima was in a class by itself, the ultimate expression of death and mayhem for the sake of death and mayhem to be found in the

The greatest vulnerability the Japanese endured was the complete absence of groundwater on Iwo Jima. The entire supply for 23,000 defenders had to be collected during rainstorms, then stored in numerous concrete cisterns, both in the cave system and on the surface. Once the Americans figured out what these round concrete structures were used for, they became prime targets for air, naval gunfire, artillery, and infantry attacks. A large number of captives arrived in American hands solely in search of water, and thirst-crazed defenders often killed themselves or were driven to break discipline and attack in the open rather than die of thirst in their burrows. *Official USMC Photo*

Final bombardment of the island's defenses was too brief and too weak to do the damage the senior ground commanders felt Iwo Jima deserved: only three days of naval gunfire preparation were authorized, only three days of air attacks by fighters and bombers aboard CVEs, and only two days by the fast carrier air groups. Even those didn't work out: bad weather grounded the escort carrier squadrons for two days and reduced the fast carrier air groups' prelanding attacks to just one day. Seen here, a TBM light bomber is about to take off from the USS *Essex*, and a U.S. Navy destroyer beats slowly along Iwo Jima's coast to take on pinpoint targets with its 5-inch guns. *Official USN Photos*

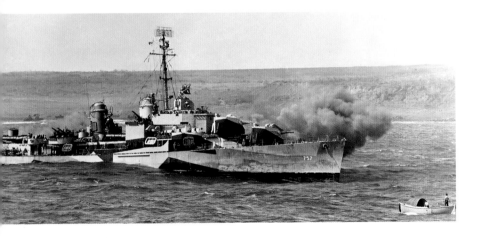

annals of the Pacific War. Improving exponentially on a "defend and die" concept first encountered by U.S. Army troops on Biak, in the Schouten Islands off New Guinea, and then by Marines at Peleliu, the island commander oversaw the construction of hundreds of bunkers, pillboxes, blockhouses, and other fighting positions as well as multistory underground command centers and underground barracks—as deep as 75 feet, and all interconnected by mid-February 1945 by 11 of a projected 17 miles of underground passageways. Holding these positions were an estimated 23,000 Imperial Army and Imperial Navy troops, many of them veterans. The hundreds of mortars and artillery pieces sprinkled throughout the defensive sectors were painstakingly preregistered to cover virtually every square yard of the island. Nearly all the defenders had been bonded into a brotherhood born of the extreme difficulties encountered during the building of bunkers and passageways underground in extreme heat laced with sulfurous fumes. Beyond that, all the defenders took an oath to fight to the death, to give no ground for any reason short of death. All questions of counterattacking the invaders were quelled; except for designated roving assault detachments, the defenders would man their positions unto death.

There was no dead ground on Iwo Jima, not one square yard that could be employed as cover with any certainty whatsoever that it was in fact cover. The only way to find dead ground was to kill for it.

D-DAY

On February 19, 1945, following a seventy-four-day air and naval bombardment that was felt by its architects to cover all the dangerous ground, two veteran regiments of the 4th Marine Division landed alongside two regiments of the new 5th Marine Division—eight battalion landing teams in all. Carrier-based aircraft, battleships, cruisers, and destroyers pummeled ground targets near and far from the landing beaches, and the destroyers established a literal curtain of fire 400 yards from the front as the first wave of amtracs climbed ashore. LCI(G) gunboats and LCI(R) rocket boats fired scores of 20mm and 40mm cannon and hundreds of rockets to suppress fire at the very last moment; then two squadrons of Marine Corsair fighter-bombers—VMF-124 and VMF-213, based aboard the USS *Essex* since December—strafed the ground just behind the beaches at such low altitude that it looked to men on the water as if they were on the ground.

Nothing happened. There was no return fire. No Japanese fired at the ships offshore, nor at the oncoming waves of amtracs, nor at Marines who were surprised to learn as their feet touched down that all of southern Iwo Jima was covered in a thick mantle of black volcanic ash—not simply black sand—that offered no purchase for their feet or their shovels.

Ahead lay another surprise: a 15-foot terrace that rose sharply from just in back of the beaches. LVT(A)s that fired their 75mm short-barrel howitzers as they landed were unable to scale this slippery slope, so many returned to the water and fired on the few suspect features the gunners could see.

Wave upon wave landed on eerily peaceful beaches. The largest force of Marines assembled to date had come to fight for Iwo Jima, and it appeared to be getting a free pass.

The descent to hell began as the lead infantry units advanced up the terrace and to points about 500 yards inland. Then the world fell in on them as prearranged fires directed by steady leaders and undertaken by skilled gunners erupted on and around every living man and mechanical aid on the landing beaches. Japanese machine gunners and riflemen hitherto hunkered down in caves or fighting positions opened fire on Marines advancing across open ground.

Only direct hits from a battleship's 14-inch or 16-inch guns could have caused this much damage to the seaward face of this rather large steel-reinforced concrete bunker. The Japanese returned fire only at the start of the prelanding bombardment, so many hidden emplacements could not be located, but a longer, more thorough, more methodical naval bombardment probably would have demolished or at least partly disabled scores or even hundreds of defensive positions that were not at all harmed. *Official USMC Photo*

Time to go. A corpsman carrying a stretcher joins his Marine comrades at the rail of their transport. *Official USMC Photo*

Ship to Shore

A sailor waves good-bye and Godspeed as a DUKW loaded with Marines begins the long journey to the beach. *Official USMC Photo*

This group of amtracs is running parallel to Iwo Jima's eastern beaches. All will head straight in as soon as they come abreast of their objective. *Official USMC Photo*

The Marines fell to the ground, looking for targets or looking after their wounds. Those who tried to dig in found that the volcanic ash could not be moved without moving back. Immediately a great hue and cry went up: send us sandbags. There was no way to dig in and no means at hand to build shelter. Marines had walked into the kill zone, and they were being killed.

There was mayhem at the beach. Infantry could manage after a fashion; there was always a way to get forward on foot, but anything with wheels sank to its axles, and even the treads on tanks and amtracs slipped and dug into the bottomless ash. In at least one case, the front wheels of a vehicle dug in as soon as they left the ramp of a landing craft, and that pinned the ramp to the beach, preventing the craft from retracting under intense mortar and artillery fire. As the day progressed, a high inshore tide just made things worse, and scores of landing craft broached in the surf and foundered.

At the front, the infantry quickly adapted to the harsh realities of Iwo Jima. Infantrymen always adapt; they are the best adapters in the world, for if they cannot or will not or even do

Behind the initial assault waves are hundreds of landing craft filled with follow-on troops, primarily machine gun and mortar squads, headquarters units, medical-surgical teams, and the first of the service troops to be sent ashore to organize the beachhead, especially the smooth transition of amphibious troops to ground infantry, and all that entails. *Official USMC Photo*

A line of troop-filled LCVPs lines up and heads directly toward Mount Suribachi. Naval gunfire vessels stand on the horizon. *Official USMC Photo*

These serious-looking youngsters have time for a few last thoughts and regrets. Soon enough, their only thoughts will be directed at closing with the enemy and surviving. *Official USMC Photo*

not adapt, they die. They couldn't dig in, and they certainly could not withdraw to the shell-struck mayhem on the beaches. So they attacked. They attacked every fighting position they could both see and reach, and then they went looking for more. In due course, they won ground, killed defenders, and advanced toward their D-day objectives. The reserve battalions were landed and thrown into the fight at the front or cleared bypassed positions behind the front. In due course, medium tanks, LVT(A)s, 75mm halftracks, and 37mm guns found their way to the front. But it was the brave infantry who took the ground from other brave infantry, all of them heedless of their lives.

At Iwo Jima's narrowest point, two companies of I/28—a new regiment composed in large part of veteran Raiders and parachutists—drove to the western shore with a costly gallantry that cannot be described in terms that have been invented yet. Both company commanders led small teams of volunteers at the heads of their units, knocked out position after position until one

continued on page 173

Beach Assault

It is 0859 hours, February 19, 1945. At the far left of the line, the amtracs carrying 1/28 to Beach Green have surged ahead of the units to their right and are just seconds away from touchdown. *Official USN Photo*

At the far right of the V Amphibious Corps beachhead, the lead assault platoons of the 4th Marine Division's 1/25 have dismounted from their amtracs and are storming Beach Blue-1. *Official USMC Photo*

Per the battalion's plan, the lead waves of 1/28 have made limited advances inland on Beach Green and have taken cover to await more troops and machine guns and mortars before commencing the drive across Iwo Jima's narrow neck, to isolate Mount Suribachi. *Official USMC Photo*

In the 5th Marine Division zone, assault platoons have pushed to the crest of the 15-foot terrace that stretches most of the way from south to north along the corps front. The leading companies of the 28th and 27th Marines will reorganize behind the terrace, then push off across the island. *Official USMC Photo*

Follow-on waves, including most infantry battalion .30-caliber medium machine guns and 81mm mortars, as well as beefed-up assault engineer teams and command-and-control elements arrive aboard LCVPs and LCMs. These troops make their way to the front line or set into predetermined positions behind the front.

Official USMC Photos

As the eight-battalion assault force clears the terrace to begin its drive inland, follow-on troops continue to land and reorganize on the beachhead. Seen here is the 5th Military Police Company, which will control vehicular traffic flow on Green, Red-1, and Red-2 as soon as routes are laid out and the trucks and jeeps begin to land.
Official USMC Photo

An amtrac blows up after being set aflame by a mortar or artillery shell. The vehicle probably had a load of ammunition aboard.
Official USMC Photo

It was bad enough that the beachhead had come under vicious fire, but then the powerful tide went to work pinning light landing craft to the surf line. Marines at Iwo Jima considered themselves lucky that there was no reef to impede landing operations, but the blessing had a dark side, for there was also no reef to mitigate the effects of a powerful inshore tide. So, after braving fire to get men and supplies ashore, many boat crews found themselves continuously under fire because their craft were unable to retract and run to safety. Many landing craft were wrecked by the surf or blown up by Japanese guns. *Official USMC Photo*

Shortly after 1000 hours, this LSM sustains two direct mortar hits as it retracts from the beach after dropping off several 5th Tank Battalion M4s. The turret of one of the M4s can be seen as it crests the ledge. *Official USMC Photo*

This medium tank, disabled before its crew could remove its fording kit, serves as a way station for infantrymen heading inland.
Official USMC Photo

A medium tank has been disabled and two amtracs have been demolished by intense mortar and artillery fire on just this narrow slice of the beachhead.
Official USMC Photo

Continued from page 166

of the captains collapsed from the effects of his mortal wounds and the other was incapacitated by merely "serious" wounds. In the wake of leaders like these, Marines who lost track of their own units joined other stragglers to take out fighting positions whose interlocking bands of fire swept over all Marines, lost and found, all along and behind the front. Marine mortars with no cover and just the rounds that could be carried to them were fired directly at targets their crews could see with their own eyes—a situation that is rare on modern battlefields.

Six of eight Marine 75mm and 105mm howitzer battalions came ashore in dribs and drabs through the long afternoon. Guns were lost when their conveyances to the beach—DUKWs from

As difficult to bear as the widespread material losses were, the human toll was devastating to unit integrity and unit morale. Though Marines fell dead and wounded in their dozens, scores, and hundreds, the front-line troops never faltered in their zeal to close with the enemy and supplant him. *Official USMC Photos*

A 4th Tank Battalion Sherman moves up to support front-line troops who have advanced inland from the Blue and Yellow beaches. In many cases, tanks were crucial to unlocking interlocked, mutually supporting defensive positions. *Official USMC Photo*

two Marine and one army amphibian truck companies—sank in the high surf or took direct hits from the pervasive bombardment, or the howitzers were hit after they were set in, or they couldn't be carried over the terrace to be set in in the first place. But slowly, using coordinates radioed in by aerial observers or forward observers at the front, or anyone at the front who could provide reliable real-time information, the howitzers in the beachhead took out positions that were holding up the ground advance. The Marine artillery and the mobile naval gunfire also took out Japanese guns, mortars, and observation posts and thus slowly cut ragged holes in the Japanese coverage of the battlefield, creating dead ground by creating dead Japanese gunners and dead Japanese mortar and artillery observers.

By 1100 hours, ten Marines from two platoons of Company B, 1/28, joined forces on their battalion's objective, the western beach at Iwo Jima's narrowest point, just 700 yards from the beachhead. Behind these brave but exhausted Marines, the 28th Marines mopped up its zone and established a continuous line across the island's narrow neck, then faced the southwestern tail

Hundreds of flamethrower teams were assigned directly to rifle squads in both divisions. Though the results of a flamethrower attack were often too gruesome to contemplate, the aggressive use of the weapon by heroic Marines was crucial to keeping the advance moving every day of the bloody battle for Iwo Jima. *Official USMC Photo*

The three 60mm mortars assigned to each Marine infantry company were employed with uncommon effect in the 28th Marines' zone, where gunners often fired their weapon while directly eyeballing the target—*not* the way mortars are usually employed. *Official USMC Photo*

This late in the Pacific War, each infantry commander was assigned a radioman packing a decent tactical radio, but the technology was limited and battery life was short. It was thus left to wire teams braving enemy fire, to knit all the components of an infantry battalion, and Marine regiment, and the divisions into a controllable body of troops capable of adjusting plans to meet ever-shifting realities. *Official USMC Photo*

Official USMC Photo

of the island, which was dominated by the forbidding height of Mount Suribachi. To the right, the 27th Marines came abreast, in places only a few yards from the western shore. But farther to the right, the 4th Marine Division was bogged down in line with the northeast–southwest taxiway of Airfield No. 1, which was to have been taken in its entirety by the 23d Marines. And farthest to the right, the 25th Marines advanced nearly to its objective, the island's shoreside quarry, but it failed by hundreds of yards to swing to the objective line anchored by the quarry. Instead of ending D-day on a line running generally east to west across the midpoint of Iwo Jima, the two Marine divisions held a northeast-to-southwest line about halfway across the southern half of the island—less than half the ground they had planned to take. Estimates place American D-day casualties at nearly 550 killed and more than 1,800 wounded or otherwise incapacitated.

SURIBACHI

By dusk on D-day, the 5th Marine Division's 28th Marines had traversed from Beach Green, on the V Amphibious Corps extreme left flank, all the way across Iwo's narrow neck. By dawn on February 20, the regiment, composed in large part of former parachutists and some Raiders, faced in two directions: the battered 1st Battalion faced north in a blocking position, and 3/28 faced south, toward Mount Suribachi, the regimental objective. Until the 556-foot-high volcano was in Marine hands, the 28th Marines would fight a battle distinct from VAC's northward drive.

The terrain to the south of the 28th Marines line was largely open, strewn with large boulders thrown out by the volcano, impeded by gullies and folds, and guarded by hundreds of bunkers, pillboxes, and other fighting emplacements. The mountain itself was isolated, brooding, and completely dominant above the land approaches.

As other units of the 5th Marine Division arrived ashore, 1/28 was put into regimental reserve, and the rest of the regiment jumped off at 0830, with 2/28 on the right (west) and 3/28 on the left. The plan was to isolate the mountain and its 1,600-man garrison, then attack uphill to the summit.

It was chilly and drizzling when the attack opened with a carrier strike that included napalm, bombs, and rockets, then a bombardment by Marine 105mm howitzers (3/13), destroyers, and LCI(R)s. A designated destroyer to the west was placed at the direct disposal of gunfire coordinators with 2/28, and a minelayer to the east did the same for 3/28.

The southern portion of Iwo Jima as seen from a heavy bomber during the long prelanding aerial bombardment. While the rest of VAC moved on the airfield, Motoyama Airfield No. 1, the 28th Marines crossed the island at the narrow neck and wheeled left, toward Suribachi. *Official USAAF Photo*

A carrier-based TBM light bomber overflies the open area between Beach Green and Suribachi. Note that the air is hazy with smoke from bombs and guns. Note also the sandbagged structures going up in the near distance. These appear to be for 3/13's 105mm howitzers. *Official USMC Photo*

A 105mm howitzer trained directly on Suribachi. The gun pit is lined with lumber and sandbags to hold back drifting volcanic ash and sand. *Official USMC Photo*

A rocket truck, still considered an experimental system and deployed in small numbers on late-war battlefields, was a deadly area weapon. Though each rocket was inaccurate, the cumulative effect of an entire sheaf from just one truck could be devastating. The telltale dust cloud that rose when the sheaf was fired meant the truck had to be moved swiftly to avoid counterfire. The Japanese were so swift getting on target that rockets were eventually fired remotely. Trucks were lost, but fewer crewmen died. *Official USMC Photo*

This .30-caliber medium machine gun from one of the nine infantry companies charged with taking Suribachi has been set into an overwatch position. The machine gunners beat up ground in advance of an advance by riflemen or attempted to suppress fire from known emplacements. *Official USMC Photo*

As soon as they stepped off, the Marines faced terrific fire from scores of emplacements, many heretofore silent, or at least uncharted. Guns, large and small, blasted the attackers. Thanks to splendid observation from the heights, the gunnery was dead on. Eight 5th Tank Battalion Shermans behind the lines were harried from one place to another to yet another by spot-on fire as their crews attempted to transfer fuel and ammunition from damaged tanks.

Gains through the morning of D+1 were 50 to 70 yards. At 1100 hours, the eight tanks were committed, and 37mm guns and 75mm halftracks were pushed forward to ranges down to pointblank. Close teamwork was required to destroy each emplacement in the regiment's path. Typically, a flamethrower team worked forward with an infantry squad as a machine gun or other suppressive weapon reached for an embrasure to keep the defenders' heads down. When ready, the flamethrower operator (sometimes several) stepped up and fired several bursts. Then he stood aside as the infantrymen closed on the position to toss hand grenades. The infantry fired into the position through the embrasures, then perhaps a demolitions assault team worked forward to blow up the emplacement. When it was possible, flame tanks were used, or maybe 75mm halftracks.

By 1700 hours, 2/28 and 3/28 had advanced about 200 yards at the cost of 29 killed and 133 wounded. Along the way the infantry and their supports killed at least 73 Japanese and blew up or otherwise neutralized approximately forty emplacements of all sizes and descriptions. The Marines also located and cut the main communications cable between the commander of the Suribachi defensive sector and higher headquarters.

Bombs, artillery, armor-piercing rounds, rockets, machine guns . . . it was all good, but in the end, men armored in shirts had to approach the scores of sheltering caves, bunkers, pillboxes, and dugouts to deal with the defenders, often at no more than arm's length. Satchel charges and other explosive devices were placed in any position located by the infantry assault teams, occupied or not. *Official USMC Photos*

As night fell, the Japanese on Suribachi fired signal flares to request that artillery and mortar fire be placed on the attackers, who ended the day in positions well short of the base of the mountain. The request was met with an ongoing barrage as heavy as the one fired during the first night of the battle.

At dawn on D+2, in cold rain and high winds, the 28th Marines hunkered down as heavy preparatory fires screamed overhead against known emplacements and designated areas. Just before the scheduled 0825 resumption of the ground attack, forty carrier fighters and bombers attacked to within a scary 100 yards of the infantry with guns, rockets, and bombs. The infantry, now including 1/28 in column of companies on the extreme left, jumped off on schedule but without tank support, due to refueling problems. Naval gunfire was placed as needed ahead of the troops.

Gains were minimal with 75mm halftracks until 1100 hours, when 37mm guns and several rocket trucks were committed. As a result, 1/28 reached the base of the mountain at about noon.

In the regimental center, 3/28 hit an immovable barrier when it jumped off, but at-first-tiny inroads spread, and by 1100 hours the battalion was making strides. The first Japanese

It took some doing at the outset of the Suribachi battles to organize ammunition and fuel resupplies, but seven or eight medium tanks from Company C, 5th Tank Battalion, were usually on hand to bolster organized pushes toward the base of the volcano. In addition to playing the role of mobile armored pillboxes, the tanks wielded their 75mm guns as especially useful antiemplacement weapons. *Official USMC Photo*

counterattack of the battle was beaten back, and then the thinned and perhaps demoralized opposition was more easily overcome. By 1400 hours 3/28 had drawn abreast of 1/28 at the base of Suribachi. On the far right, 2/28 was held to very small gains for most of the day in the face of unremitting heavy fire, but it eventually bulled through to join its sister battalions on a wide semicircle at the base of the mountain. For gains ranging between 500 and 1,000 yards, the 28th Marines had given up 34 dead and 153 wounded—adding up with previous casualties to 25 percent losses in three days.

After the advance was halted, roving Marines poured gasoline into fissures from which they could hear voices and set the fuel ablaze to the accompaniment of screams and cooking-off ammunition. This was about as brutal as infantry warfare can get. The Japanese to the north once again contributed artillery and mortar fire that forced the Marine hunters to seek cover.

February 22 dawned miserable and rainy. Overnight the rain had turned the volcanic ash to mush that infiltrated the workings of many weapons, thus impeding the rate of fire the 28th Marines could put on the many targets that still lay to the front. The weather kept air support grounded on the carrier decks, and visibility from warships' gun directors was

Only a few dozen Suribachi defenders died in the open, mainly those who sought to flee north. The only known print of this photo has been damaged. *Official USMC Photo*

impaired. On the plus side, after two days of resupply fiascoes, seven fully fueled and armed Shermans were on hand at the front when the assault recommenced.

In the center, 3/28 lurched forward against Suribachi's northern face, then dispatched a patrol eastward to the island's southern extremity. A patrol from 2/28 advanced to the same feature via a westward route, so the volcano was more or less surrounded. Most of the regiment spent the day dressing its lines and methodically taking out emplacements around the base—so much so that the defensive establishment was reduced to an estimated 300 survivors by nightfall. A sergeant from 3/28 returned from a lone-wolf foray partway up the northern slope to report no signs of the defenders. Even though this intimated an opportunity to take some ground quickly and cheaply, the regimental commander decided it was too late in the day for 3/28 to advance and then properly dig it in.

The assault on the volcano itself jumped off on the morning of D+4, February 23, 1945. There was only one practical route—up the northern face—and so only 2/28 was designated to step off. The other two battalions scoured their zones for fighting emplacements they had thus far missed.

THE FLAG

A four-man patrol from Company F climbed all the way to the summit, where it encountered an unmanned machine gun strongpoint at the rim of the crater. A week of intense bombardment on these heights had made a tangle of blasted bunkers, pillboxes, and strewn weapons, gear, and supplies. There was no sign of a living being.

When word arrived of the easy passage to the summit, 2/28 mounted a forty-five-man patrol to secure it. Traveling up Suribachi with the patrol was an American flag and a Marine photographer. The patrol arrived at the summit unscathed and overcame a few Japanese stragglers there. As soon as the Marines had possession, the flag was raised on an iron pipe. Later, another squad of Marines was sent to the summit with a larger flag, a Marine movie cameraman, a Marine still photographer, and a civilian news photographer. The civilian, Joe Rosenthal, took three photos as the second flag was raised. One of his photos made the event immortal and bound together a war-frayed American population for the final surge to achieve victory in World War II.

✵   ✵   ✵

continued on page 185

The first U.S. flag to fly atop Suribachi was carried to the summit by a forty-five-man patrol built around the 3d Platoon of Company E, 2/28. Its appearance caused a solid cheer to arise above the sound of the battle. *Leatherneck Magazine by Staff Sergeant Louis R. Lowery*

This photo, taken from the movie film, shows five Marines and a corpsman from Company E's 2d Platoon as they prepare to raise the larger, second flag. *Official USMC Photo by Sergeant William Genaust*

Opposite: The Flag-Raising at Iwo Jima.
Joe Rosenthal

Right: Once the second flag was up and the first flag had been lowered, the nearly sixty combat troops atop Suribachi spread out to defend the summit from Japanese still moving freely in caves and within bunkers and pillboxes. *Official USMC Photo by Private Robert R. Campbell*

Below: Scores of lives were not sacrificed simply for a place to put a flag. This view was why Suribachi figured so prominently in VAC's invasion plan. In short order, observation posts, artillery spotting aids, and such wonders as radar lined the northern limit of the summit. *Official USMC Photo*

Iwo Jima looking south to north. VAC's primary D-day objective, Motoyama Airfield No. 1, and a line stretching across the island above the east-west runway took days and involved the commitment of two reinforced regiments of the 3d Marine Division to secure. In the end, for VAC's northward drive, the three Marine divisions lined up all the way across the island: the 4th Marine Division on the right, most of the 3d Marine Division in the center, and the 5th Marine Division on the left.
National Archives and Records Administration

The front lines. Ahead lies wide-open ground these Marines know they will have to traverse; there's no other way to get from here to there and no room for spiffy maneuvers. It's just straight ahead all the way. *Official USMC Photo*

Continued from page 181
PACIFYING IWO

It took five days and the commitment in the center of the 3d Marine Division, less one infantry regiment, for the rest of the V Amphibious Corps (VAC) troops to reach approximately their D-day objective line. The fighting, which was similar to but far more intense than the drive on Suribachi, was a meatgrinder. Thousands of Marines were killed or wounded. There was no finesse, no elegant battlefield solutions; only sledgehammer tactics worked, only brute force prevailed.

Slow, steady advances over increasingly rough terrain ensued. Two-thirds of Iwo Jima was in Marine hands by March 1. The rough terrain actually made the job easier as firm ground and natural cover became ample, but it also provided the Japanese with ample defensive possibilities. Nonetheless, by then, American artillery, naval gunfire, and air support had winnowed the Japanese artillery, mortars, and machine guns and broken unit cohesion. No place on Iwo Jima was ever safe throughout and even after the long, grueling battle, but a lot of the island was safer than it had been in the first week.

By March 11, the organized defense had been squeezed into two pockets, then pushed back until the island was declared secure on March 16. Mopping up by an army occupation force continued for months, and stragglers and organized assault teams evaded capture and threw in raids where they could.

Killed and wounded Americans numbered 6,821 and 19,217, respectively. Iwo Jima was America's bloodiest Pacific War battle.

continued on page 195

A meeting of troop leaders before an infantry unit jumps off into the attack. These officers and noncommissioned officers are getting the attack plan straight in their heads by consulting maps of the objective area. *Official USMC Photo*

A platoon leader or squad leader conveys directions to his subordinates as the time for preparations winds down. *Official USMC Photo*

Heavily burdened Marines charge across open ground under fire. The radioman at far right is firing his rifle. *Official USMC Photo*

Official USMC Photo

PS.33:9

I JW.
5:12,13

This Marine was shot dead as he humped ammunition across fireswept ground. *Official USMC Photo*

As the turret of the flame tank traverses from right to left to singe a long swath of hostile ground, Marine infantrymen use the oily, black smoke to cover their maneuvers. *Official USMC Photo*

An 81mm mortar squad readies its ammunition supply for an upcoming fire mission. *Official USMC Photo*

A 60mm mortar gunner from Company K, 3/9, hangs a round at the muzzle of the cannon, waiting for the order to open fire. *Official USMC Photo*

These 5th Marine Division infantrymen spend a few minutes resting in the relative safety of a curve in the road. *Official USMC Photo*

It's time to move out again. *Official USMC Photo*

A flamethrower operator and the men around him were killed by a direct mortar or artillery hit that breached the fuel tanks. *Official USMC Photo*

North of Motoyama Airfield No. 2, VAC ground troops faced successive ridges and formations of volcanic rocks honeycombed with improved natural caves and hundreds of manmade emplacements often connected by hidden passageways cut into the basaltic rock. There are at least seven cave mouths visible in this narrow view. *Official USMC Photo*

Once located, each cave had to be knocked out by the weapons in hand, but even then there was no assurance that it wasn't going to be remanned by Japanese soldiers using unseen entries tens or even hundreds of yards away. No *sign* of life did not preclude that there was hostile life waiting to kill or maim the unwary Marine. *Official USMC Photo*

The BAR-man at right and two riflemen are either ready to fire or actually laying down suppressive fire as other Marines approach a cave mouth atop a hill in northern Iwo Jima. *Official USMC Photo*

This Japanese soldier was killed on open ground in the 5th Marine Division zone west of Motoyama Airfield No. 2. The weapon is a 6.5mm Nambu light machine gun. *Official USMC Photo*

It became increasingly difficult to make effective use of VAC's three tank battalions as the battle moved deeper and steeper into hilly terrain, but the Sherman's 75mm main gun was an ideal cave buster if it could be brought to bear. As the Sherman's main gun obliterates a cave at pointblank range, the accompanying infantrymen, from 3/28, move across the open ground with impunity. *Official USMC Photo*

A very brave Marine stands tall on the skyline to lob a hand grenade at a Japanese emplacement. By the late stages of the battle only the brave and the lucky were left. *Official USMC Photo*

A bazookaman carefully lines his sights up on a cave. The solid punch of the 2.36-inch shaped-charge rocket he will fire is sufficient to penetrate a tank hull or obliterate many caves. *Official USMC Photo*

Marine riflemen close in on a variety of Japanese emplacements at various stages of the battle. By this phase of the war, each Marine was minutely trained to take part in such cooperative ventures of shared risk. *Official USMC Photos*

In the end, the only way to be sure the Japanese manning a cave, bunker, or pillbox were quelled was to burn them out. And the only way to be sure an emplacement could not be reoccupied was to blow it up.
Official USMC Photos

Official USMC Photo

Left: Dinah Might, the first B-29 to put in at Iwo, landed with engine problems on March 4, 1945, a little before the former Motoyama Airfield No. 1 was declared open. Without Iwo, her crew might have made it to the Marianas, or it might have perished on the way. In the end, most of the men saved in this landing later died over Japan. *Official USMC Photo*

By war's end, the runways at Iwo had been completely hardtopped and hardstands had been built for aircraft dispersal. By then, Marianas-based B-24 and B-29 groups shuttling to and from Japan had been routinely staging through Iwo for several months, and a Marine PBJ radar-guided night-bomber squadron was based on Iwo to conduct antishipping missions over southern Japan. *Official USAAF Photo*

Continued from page 185
WEIGHING THE COST

Airfield rehabilitation got under way close on the heels of the capture of Airfield No. 1 in late February. The task was threefold: to base Marine tactical squadrons assigned to help over the battlefield and isolate nearby garrisons; to base long-range army air forces fighters that would escort Marianas-based B-29s over Japan; and to serve as an emergency base for B-29s with malfunctions or battle damage and that might not otherwise have been able to get back to the Marianas. In some circles, it is noted that Iwo Jima serviced 2,251 B-29s by the end of the war, and this figure is converted to a claim that the lives of 24,761 crewmen were saved—a number just a little below the number of casualties sustained by VAC in taking the island. Others point out that many

Official USMC Photo

of the B-29s that landed at Iwo did so because it was there, not because they direly needed to set down there. A response to that is that Iwo-based fighters operating over Japan saved hundreds of bombers from being shot down there. And so forth.

Were the lives of airmen saved by Iwo's being there worth the lives expended and ruined in the taking of Iwo? It's an argument between emotions; there is no objective answer.

SUMMING UP

Taken on its own merits, Iwo Jima was a meatgrinder smashed over time by a blunt instrument at exceedingly high cost. As was the case in every bloody battle in the Pacific and, indeed, in most wars, very little comes between the bravery of men who did their duty and the heartfelt thanks of a grateful nation. Moreover, a single photograph snapped by a civilian war correspondent at the summit of Mount Suribachi on February 23, 1945, has served from that very week onward as a palpably living symbol of the bravery that rose upon every square inch that was touched by an American boot during that bloodiest of Pacific battles—indeed, in all Pacific War battles.

Official USMC Photo

Part III

OKINAWA

★ ★ ★ ★ ★

Marines assault Okinawa over the bow of an amphibian tractor. *Official USMC Photo*

INTRODUCTION

THE AMERICAN CAMPAIGN IN THE WESTERN PACIFIC from late 1944 to mid-1945 was a violent undertaking at every turn. The Japanese had been relentlessly pushed back throughout 1944. Except for Japan itself, there was very little left for them to defend. They had clearly lost their war of conquest in the Pacific and East Asia, but they could not bring themselves to settle gracefully; their warrior code prevented them from doing anything less than standing their ground—especially their homeland—and dying.

By late March 1945, the pathway to invasion of the southernmost major island of the Japanese archipelago, Kyushu, had been secured but for one necessary stepping stone the American forces needed to support its tactical air effort leading up to and overhead the invasion of Japan in the autumn of 1945. The seizure of Okinawa and its airfields was vital to the land-based strategic bombing campaign that would precede and support the invasion of Japan and for close-in basing of the scores of Marine and U.S. Army Air Forces tactical air units that were slated to guard the approach of the Kyushu invasion fleet and operate over the beachheads in the face of anticipated fanatical Japanese air defenses.

A firefight in central Okinawa. *Official USMC Photo*

Marines of the veteran 1st and 6th Marine divisions and tens of thousands of battle-tested soldiers of the U.S. Army's XXIV Corps assigned to seize Okinawa beginning on April 1, 1945, saw nothing but weeks or even months of heavy fighting ahead as they sailed to confront the largest Japanese defense force deployed on any island Americans invaded in the Pacific.

The fast battleship USS *Idaho* unleashes her nine 16-inch naval rifles against targets behind L-day beaches slated for assault by the U.S. Tenth Army's XXIV Corps and III Amphibious Corps. *Official USN Photo*

7

ON THE BEACH AND IN THE NORTH

April 1–April 20, 1945

THE STRATEGIC SITUATION

When two Marine and two U.S. Army divisions landed abreast on Okinawa on L-day, April 1, 1945, they faced an estimated 155,000 Japanese ground, air, and naval troops holding an immense island on which an estimated 500,000 civilians lived in cities, towns, and villages. Okinawa was to be, in every way, vast when compared to any other operation undertaken by Allied forces in the Pacific War under U.S. Navy command. Indeed, using mainly divisions that had undertaken island-hopping operations in the southern and central Pacific since mid-1942, the U.S. Pacific Fleet stood up the Tenth U.S. Army, consisting of III Amphibious Corps (IIIAC) and XXIV Army Corps—the largest land command ever assembled under the direct control of the U.S. Navy.

To those Japanese who thought the war was winnable, Okinawa was the last chance. The island lay within 350 miles—easy single-engine flight distance—from the Japanese homeland and was, by American design, to be the base from which the southernmost home island, Kyushu, was to be pummeled to dust ahead of the expected follow-on invasion. Anything short of complete victory over Allied air, naval, and ground forces spelled doom for Japan, but no such victory was remotely in the cards. Thus, by Japanese lights, Okinawa was and could be no more than a delaying battle of attrition on a grand scale. The few Japanese who knew that Japan's war effort was in extremis were content to fight on Okinawa simply for reasons of honor, for all military logic pointed to the same dismal conclusion: Japan was vanquished in

The commanding officer of the 6th Marine Division's 2d Battalion, 29th Marines (2/29) inspects his men on the day before the landing. Note how young these Marines are. The 29th Marines was to be the III Amphibious Corps reserve during the initial phase of the battle for Okinawa. *Official USMC Photo*

Heavily laden Marines nimbly cross-deck from an LCVP to an amphibian tractor (amtrac) for the final lap to the invasion beaches. *Official USMC Photo*

Though crowded tightly into the troop compartment of an amtrac bearing down on the beach, these 1st Marine Division infantrymen appear to be alone with their thoughts. *Official USMC Photo*

all but name as soon as the first U.S. Army Air Forces B-29 very-heavy strategic bombers left the ground in the Marianas, as soon as American carrier aircraft hit targets in Japan at will, as soon as even twin-engine bombers could strike Japanese ports from Iwo Jima, as soon as Japan dared not move a warship or cargo vessel from a port in any part of the shrinking empire for fear it would be sunk by an American submarine. By April 1, 1945, all those events were taking place routinely.

THE DEFENSES

Although the Japanese commanders counted 155,000 defenders, their forces were of widely uneven abilities, and there were not nearly enough troops in total to cover the ground the way 23,000 troops had covered Iwo Jima. Rather than dilute their power in an effort to cover all the ground, the Japanese commanders on Okinawa concentrated the bulk of their forces in a number of contiguous sectors that offered the best prospects for a robust,

On Beach Yellow-1, members of the 1st Marine Division's 2d Battalion, 5th Marines (2/5) exit a new LVT-4 amtrac with alacrity via the rear ramp. These Marines, including veterans of bloody Peleliu, expect to face withering fire, but no such thing happens. The beach assault on Okinawa might as well be a practice landing for all the blood that is shed. *Official USMC Photo*

Still waiting on the punch line, this platoon of hyperalert Marines has re-formed a few yards inland to await orders to advance. So far there are no battle casualties. *Official USMC Photo*

The Japanese had prepared an excellent defensive zone overlooking Beach Yellow-2, but even this stout, beautifully constructed pillbox was abandoned before the invasion began. *Official USMC Photo*

On Beach Red-3, in the 6th Marine Division zone, this 1/4 rifleman thinks he sees something that might endanger him or his buddies. He might fire a few shots, but there are few defenders—and no effective opposition—within miles of the beachhead. *Official USMC Photo*

attritional defense. The northern half of the island was virtually conceded, and the southern half was turned into four extremely tough hedgehog defense sectors. The proportion of artillery and mortars to infantry was the highest encountered in the Pacific War.

L-DAY

The new 6th Marine Division (the veteran 1st Provisional Marine Brigade plus the 29th Marines and attachments) landed over the northernmost beaches on the western side of Okinawa a little south of the island's midpoint. It was to strike across the island, then turn north to pacify a little more than half of Okinawa on its own. To the right, the 1st Marine Division, in its fourth island invasion of the war, also was to strike across the island, then turn to as part of the Tenth Army reserve. The XXIV Corps, composed initially of two U.S. Army infantry divisions plus supports, landed side by side in the southern half of the Tenth Army beachhead, then pivoted south to cover the width of the island. Also on April 1, the IIIAC reserve, the 2d Marine Division, made a feint toward a set of beaches in southeastern Okinawa. This feint was in line with where the Japanese predicted the main landing would take place, so for once a feint actually held large numbers of defenders in place looking the wrong way. Other units, including the Fleet Marine Force, Pacific, Reconnaissance Battalion, were assigned objectives elsewhere in the Ryukyu Islands, most of which were taken or at least assaulted before L-day on Okinawa.

Immediate objectives were Yontan and Kadena airdromes, in the IIIAC and XXIV Corps zones, respectively. As soon as these airfields could be brought to operational status, combat-support aircraft would operate from them. Also, many aircraft carriers, large and small, would remain on station off Okinawa for as long as their air groups were needed. The early-phase land-based aviation component was a Marine command named the Tactical Air Force, consisting of several air groups of the 2d Marine Aircraft Wing composed of fighters and light bombers. Marine fighter squadrons based aboard fleet carriers and several new Marine carrier air groups (fighters and torpedo bombers) based aboard escort carriers would be available throughout the land operation.

The landings were made against zero opposition and with almost no casualties. Far from going into a state of optimism, however, the many veterans in the assault force realized that a very hard road lay before them, that the Japanese had chosen to dig deep and fight on their own terms.

Then the word goes out: advance to all L-day objectives. On Beach Blue-1, at the juncture between the 1st and 6th Marine divisions, an orderly file of Marines from 2/7 uses a path through the shell-damaged seawall to begin the advance inland. *Official USMC Photo*

Advancing across a landscape turned inside out by a harsh preinvasion bombardment, these front-line Marines have begun to relax and pick up the pace as they become used to an unopposed advance from the beaches. *Official USMC Photo*

Screened by two regimental combat teams advancing rapidly in combat formation against null opposition, a column of troops from the veteran 1st Marines trudges inland along a well-built roadway. The 1st Marines had been in the lead at Cape Gloucester and Peleliu, but at Okinawa it is the 1st Marine Division's reserve regiment, an overdue respite that might have had more meaning if there had been any opposition for the sister regiments to overcome. *Official USMC Photo*

An LVT(A) armored amtrac from the 1st Armored Amphibian Tractor Battalion crosses a Marine-occupied ditch at the outer edge of Yontan Airdrome midmorning of L-day. *Official USMC Photo*

Infantrymen from the 6th Marine Division's 4th Marines keep pace with an advancing LVT(A) within the wide, open Yontan Airfield zone. Light to moderate opposition in and around the air base was centered on several machine gun emplacements that were rapidly overrun. Dark smoke rises from an underground fuel tank that has been set on fire. *Official USMC Photo*

Yontan Airdrome fell by midmorning, after Marines over-came very light opposition along the juncture of the 1st and 6th Marine divisions. Reinforcements moved to fill gaps that developed due to rapid advances by the 22d, 4th, and 7th Marine regiments (22d Marines, etc.). Elements of the 1st Division captured an intact bridge across a stream at the IIIAC–XXIV Corps boundary and overcame hastily built field fortifications all across the division front. Divisional and IIIAC artillery battalions landed routinely, and many batteries were able to provide on-call fire support by 1530 hours.

The IIIAC advance halted between 1600 and 1700 hours to avoid the creation of more gaps and to help the Marines on the IIIAC far right maintain contact with the left army division, whose left flank outpaced the 1st Marine Division's right-flank unit by several hundred yards. The halt also gave artillery units outpaced by the rapid advance time to move forward and register night defensive fires.

Basically, all of L-day's headaches arose from the light-to-nonexistent defensive effort, and not the usual spate of battle problems. Both airdromes, Kadena and Yontan, were firmly in

American hands by nightfall, and engineers were already at work to get them operational in the shortest possible time.

JUGGERNAUT

While by no means a romp, the days that followed on L-day were nearly bloodless. Enemy troops were encountered here and there as the two Marine divisions swallowed up miles of territory against, at most, desultory opposition. Captives proved to be second- and third-rate troops, mostly technicians and other noncombatants drafted into ad hoc defensive units, lightly armed and miserably trained. Also, many thousands of Okinawan civilians turned themselves in to Marines, to be passed along to temporary stockades in the safe rear. The

The opening moves in the conquest of Okinawa took place in beautiful weather, and the relative lack of combat maintained the beauty of the heavily settled, heavily cultivated portions of the island overrun by both Marine divisions. Once the advances settled down to fairly bloodless routine, not many Marines concerned themselves with the impact that row after row of high hills separated by wide, flat valleys were going to have if the Japanese dug in and stubbornly stood their ground. *Official USMC Photo*

Okinawa's traditional burial vaults posed a particularly vexing challenge as the Marine offensive bit into undefended territory. Each vault was constructed of concrete, and each could be turned into a fortress by even one or two determined defenders. Each vault had to be approached warily, and when some turned out to be hiding places for ammunition, supplies, records, and even headquarters of various sorts—not to mention defended by determined rear guards, snipers, and stragglers—each had to be combed thoroughly by brave men moving from the light of day to the dank, dark interiors. The same held true for Okinawa's many thousands of masonry buildings as well as for concrete and masonry defensive emplacements and bunkers that had been built, supplied, and manned before the decision to consolidate the defenders in the southern half of the island. *Official USMC Photos*

most hard-pressed Marine units were engineers, then supply troops. Many roads were barely discernible paths, so they had to be engineered for modern traffic, and many bridges had to be built over gullies and other breaks in the terrain. Many of the bridges in the IIIAC zone had to be replaced in the wake of a robust Japanese demolition campaign. Even where the road net was adequate by modern standards, it was difficult to push supplies forward to the rapidly advancing ground units; they moved ahead thousands of yards a day and were constantly on the brink of outrunning their dumps. It was difficult, also, for artillery units to keep pace with the advance, and the infantry had a difficult time maintaining contact with flank units because the advance tended to broaden an already broad front. By April 3—L+2—the Marine divisions were on ground slated to fall on L+15.

A picture slowly emerged from prisoner interrogations. The main Japanese effort had gone into deeply fortifying the southern portion of the island. XXIV Corps ran into the outlying positions on April 4, on the phase line established for L+10. But Marines were oriented east and north, and rapidly swallowing square miles of lightly defended ground each day. Before the two Marine divisions could join the fight in the south, they had to secure the rest of the island.

One unexpected factor that limited the speed of the advance in many places was infrastructure that was both aged and underbuilt for the prolonged use by long lines of heavy modern military equipment. Despite dangerous cracking in the concrete archway, the bridge carrying the 1st Marine Division M7 assault gun across one of Okinawa's myriad streams on April 4 was, for a time at least, up to the challenge. But the 1st Tank Battalion M4 plunged through the roadway of another rural bridge even though the decking was constructed of steel-reinforced concrete. There was no way to know how much abuse a particular bridge or section of roadway could absorb before giving way, and the advance, which was transformed in only two or three days from cautious disbelief to impatient bravado, proceeded at top speed until this or that bill came due. *Official USMC Photos*

There were three Marine engineer battalions ashore as the IIIAC dual advances gained steam, and a plethora of work that stretched the ingenuity and patience of men who knew exactly how capable these premier combat-support organizations were. Beyond inadequate and failing infrastructure was willful destruction by Japanese sappers who had months and even years to plan the most vexatious approach to delaying the Marine juggernauts to the east and north—or, as often happened, a matter of minutes to plant a charge that might hold up the advance for hours. The Marine engineers had brilliant solutions to all such problems, beginning with the all-purpose span-any-gap Bailey bridge, a life-scale Erector set whose component design was certainly up to bridging almost any gap in Okinawa's rural road net. A basic Bailey bridge could be assembled, thrown, and completed by an engineer platoon in a few hours, but some bridges required days of work. The ingenious system was wide enough and strong enough to carry an M4 medium tank from solid roadway to solid roadway. If a bridge was not the right solution, then a bypass could be installed, often in a few hours. *Official USMC Photos*

Mines—sometimes purpose-built, sometimes improvised from artillery shells and aerial bombs—were another significant factor limiting the advance. Caution over mines was often thrown to the winds by the advancing combat vanguards, but sooner or later engineers had to sweep the roadways and gingerly dispose of embedded explosive devices. *Official USMC Photo*

By April 4, the 1st Marine Division had completed its cross-island advance and had thus run out of objectives. It turned to scouring land already in its hands and building up its logistical base. By then, cut-off Japanese troops in the IIIAC zone had begun to coalesce into what Marines eventually characterized as guerrilla forces that lived off the land in wild areas and exploited opportunities to attack patrols and rear-area facilities. Such forces also appeared in the rear of the 6th Marine Division. These so-called guerrillas had to be painstakingly tracked by Marine units far better suited for intense modern conflict than pacification. Fortunately, though they were well motivated, the Japanese guerrillas also were not trained for such operations either, and they were easily hunted down if they showed

themselves. To help quell civilian complicity in the enervating guerrilla operation, several thousand Okinawan males were interned in camps beginning on April 11. Tenth Army eventually clamped down on all civilians and filled eight internment camps in the IIIAC zone with Okinawans of all ages and both sexes. This seemed to end the problem of civilian aid to guerrilla operations, but guerrillas continued to operate in diminished circumstances.

The modern army of which IIIAC was a part was a wired army, its diverging components bound together mainly by phone lines. As fast as the leading combat elements were able to advance in a day was as fast as communications wiremen had to keep them tied into higher headquarters. Marine wire teams had never before had to maintain the pace that challenged them in central and northern Okinawa throughout April 1945, but they were equipped and motivated to do so. Note in the second photo that the 6th Tank Battalion M4 is passing beneath at least a dozen lines of communications wire. *Official USMC Photos*

The 6th Marine Division continued to drive north—literally driven on tanks and other vehicles. One reconnaissance force advanced 14 miles unopposed, then turned back to the main body. The 6th Engineer Battalion had a tough time widening and improving roads and replacing or bracing bridges at such a pace. On April 9, supplies began to come ashore on beaches much closer to the 6th Division front, and the 1st Armored Amtrac Battalion was committed to provide direct artillery support because the 15th Marines artillery battalions had such a bad time keeping pace with the infantry.

It took the 6th Marine Division until April 13 to locate a well-led, competent, and powerful Japanese force—on Mount Yae Take, in extreme northern Okinawa. A four-day battle involving Marine Air and artillery and naval gunfire support reduced the Japanese force of about fifteen hundred and opened the door for the final northern push, which was completed on April 20. So far on Okinawa, the 6th Marine Division's losses numbered 207 killed, 757 wounded, and 6 missing against an estimated two thousand Japanese troops killed.

☆   ☆   ☆

continued on page 224

Back at the beachhead, thousands of Marines and sailors struggled mightily to keep the advancing front-line units and follow-on support units supplied with their every requirement, be it bullets or motor oil or rations or communications wire. Shown here on April 10 as an example of beachhead development is Beach Yellow-1, over which 2/5 had landed on L-day. Thanks to terrific advance data gathering based on hydrographic surveys and three years of hard, painful experience, a floating causeway had been installed so that supplies and equipment could be offloaded directly from cargo ships and transports anchored offshore. A network of roadways had been built and numerous dumps had been created, all in very short order. The beach operation added up to a smoothly running whole that fulfilled all its goals, but the troops at the front were soon running short of rations and other essentials because the swift advance simply outpaced the trucks that had to convey it all from the beaches; the time it took for a large but finite number of trucks to carry loads to the front and then deadhead back to the beachhead was well beyond the most sanguine estimates for the conquest of fully half of the immense island. *Official USMC Photo*

When the roadway that trucks could use gave way to unimproved paths that led to where the infantry had to operate, the infantry had to fetch whatever could be carried by however many front-line troops could be spared and humped over and through whatever obstacles those men encountered. *Official USMC Photos*

In some places, the IIIAC juggernaut *was* a juggernaut; every vehicle in the inventory was pressed into service to carry infantrymen from town to town, stopping only to check out features selected by their commanders for special attention or to take on Japanese stragglers who dared to defy them. Nevertheless, whenever the spearhead stopped or stalled, the entire roadbound mass of traffic ground to a halt, creating hours-long delays when only minutes-long halts reverberated back along the limited axes of advance. Sometimes hoofing it outpaced the motor columns. *Official USMC Photos*

It wasn't all a cakewalk, it wasn't all bloodless. Seen here, on April 11 and April 13, respectively, small groups of Marine infantrymen diverged from road convoys or alighted from them to take on defenders. In the first photo, Marines close in on Japanese soldiers who have opened fire from a stand of trees. In the second, Marines burn down a farm building around a stubborn sniper. *Official USMC Photos*

The Japanese soldier seen here was the first prisoner to fall into the hands of the 22d Marines, on April 5. After his wound was treated by the corpsman at left, linguists gathered around the prisoner to reassure and question him. Japanese servicemen received no training regarding comportment as captives—because capture was unthinkable to them—so they usually told interrogators whatever they knew, as long as they were treated humanely. *Official USMC Photo*

Throughout the long lead-up to Okinawa, most Japanese captives fell into American hands while they were incapacitated by injuries, or because they were literally dying from starvation or thirst. The group in this photo, including the youth at the far right, who might be a local, have voluntarily surrendered. Presumably they are technicians or some other category of noncombatants.

Official USMC Photo

Two of these three captives are definitely substandard troops. The tall man at the right is a twenty-eight-year-old Korean noncombatant labor conscript, while the others are (center) a nineteen-year-old Japanese and (left) a seventeen-year-old Japanese—not young children, as they appear. They say a lot about Japan's ability to fill out its army in mid-1945. Nonetheless, even though fit Okinawan men were hastily conscripted in 1945 to fill out even some highly respected combat units, no one should mistake these scowling diminutive teens for the typical, tough front-line soldiers the Japanese had committed to the real defense in the south. Conscripts such as these went to expendable third-rate and ad hoc units committed to static defenses.

Official USMC Photo

If Japanese soldiers were thin on the ground in the IIIAC area of operations, tens or hundreds of thousands of native Okinawans were encountered at every turn and stop. Some were disoriented or ill oldsters displaced from their towns and farmsteads by the rumble and roar of a modern army on the move, others were hale and hearty folks of every age and description who entered American lines to get food or seek medical treatment. Most Okinawans had little love for Japanese, who considered them racially inferior vestiges of a conquered people and who often treated them with brutal disregard. At first the Okinawan civilians had no idea what to make of the tall, wealthy-looking invaders, and vice versa. There were unfortunate episodes involving keyed-up front-line troops in accidental encounters, but word quickly went out to treat the civilians with, if not kindness or warmth, at the very least humanity. For the most part, even the most battle-hardened Marines were good-natured, good-hearted American teens looking for an idealistic outlet in the middle of a hellish and miserable episode in their lives. Treating displaced, frightened noncombatants humanely was fine with nearly all of them. *Official USMC Photos*

This photo, taken on April 15, demonstrates the advance planning that went into the role of military government for the American-occupied areas of Okinawa. The civilians, no doubt waiting to hear what will become of them, are orderly and surprisingly well turned out, and none of the Americans in view appears to be armed. *Official USMC Photo*

A Marine lieutenant checks through the pockets and gear of a Japanese soldier who was killed by the patrol the lieutenant was leading. He is searching for information that might help fit pieces of intelligence together into a clearer picture of Japanese strength, order of battle, dispositions, or even the state of Japanese industry. *Official USMC Photo*

The long drives to the east and north provided the Marines of the 1st and 6th divisions with an unexpectedly easy transition to battle. The unblooded troops gained the most, but even the remaining veterans of Cape Gloucester, Guam, and Peleliu benefited from the breaking-in period. Unit leaders were given a rare opportunity to eliminate troops who did not measure up and promote those who did not blossom until the shooting started. Combat skills and instincts can only be honed under fire. *Official USMC Photos*

Nor did experience come without cost. Three of the Marines in the squad shown here were wounded when they stepped into the firing cone of a Japanese machine gun and a nearby sniper. Mortar fire quickly blanketed the Japanese, and the wounded Marines were evacuated. *Official USMC Photo*

Marine riflemen line up for their daily dose: fragmentation and smoke grenades, and clips of .30-caliber bullets for their M1 rifles. Someone higher up the chain of command believes these Marines will need the munitions. *Official USMC Photo*

Okinawa was terrific tank country, the very best American tankers encountered in the Pacific. While the road net in rural northern Okinawa was sometimes problematic or even nonexistent, the Marine M4 tanks undertook dashes and slashes that resembled action by cavalry of old. All the Marine tanks really lacked here were Japanese tanks to fight. *Official USMC Photo*

Official USMC Photo

Thanks to a mighty effort by the 6th Engineer Battalion to rehabilitate short stretches of runway at Yontan Airdrome in less than a day, several OY spotter planes from Marine Observation Squadron 6 (VMO-6) flew in from escort carriers at about 1500 hours on April 2. The OYs immediately began to fly reconnaissance and spotting missions over IIIAC. *Official USMC Photo*

In due course, to extend their range and flight time over the front line, the OYs operated from improved stretches of roadway as close to advancing ground units as possible. *Official USMC Photo*

Continued from page 215

MARINE AIR

Elements of the 2d Marine Aircraft Wing, amply assisted by a sophisticated array of modern tools such as search, control, and weather radars; landing force air-support control units equipped with advanced radio equipment; and front-line forward air control teams played a key role in supporting ground operations *and* forestalling kamikaze and conventional air attacks on the huge fleet that seemed to be a permanent fixture off Okinawa.

On April 7, the Marine Air Group 31 (MAG-31) headquarters began to handle flight operations for its newly arrived fighter squadrons at Yontan Airfield, and MAG-33 arrived with more fighter squadrons on April 9. This relieved some of the ground-support burden on air units of the large carriers, which were increasingly drawn into a battle of attrition with kamikaze and conventional air units based in Japan and intermediate bases.

Yontan Airdrome on April 10. All three of the base's runways had been open for emergency use by the afternoon of L+2, and the flight echelons of the first permanently based Marine combat squadrons had landed with the Marine Air Group 31 (MAG-31) headquarters on April 6 and 7. *Official USMC Photo*

American air bases on Okinawa, only 350 miles from mainland Kyushu and far less from Japanese airfields in the chain of small islands between Kyushu and Okinawa, were objects of almost-around-the-clock attacks and harassment. Seen here, during the night of April 16, is a brief second of antiaircraft fire overhead Yontan. IIIAC's 1st Provisional Antiaircraft Artillery Group, whose headquarters landed on April 2, oversaw four Marine antiaircraft artillery battalions, each equipped with 90mm, 40mm, and 20mm antiaircraft weapons that were deployed around the vital beachhead area and Yontan. *Official USMC Photo*

A Marine F4U Corsair on the taxiway. The flight echelon of VMF(N)-543 (in Grumman F6F-5N night fighters) arrived at Yontan on April 6, and the flight echelons of VMF-441 (in F4Us) and VMF(N)-542 began to operate from Yontan on April 7. These units were joined on April 9 by the flight echelons of MAG-33's VMF-312, VMF-322, and VMF-323. Two other Marine air groups overseeing eight fighter squadrons and one night-fighter squadron were shipped to Okinawa in May and June. *Official USMC Photo*

F4Us, which were referred to as fighter-bombers by 1945, could carry up to eight high-velocity aerial rockets (HVARs) on wing pylons as well as one center-line bomb, usually a 500-pound high-explosive bomb or napalm. *Official USMC Photo*

Two Marine torpedo-bomber squadrons, VMTB-232 (seen here over Okinawa) and VMTB-131, were deployed to Okinawa on May 1 and May 29, respectively, the only such units to reach the island. Marine TBMs were typically used as light bombers; they carried up to 2,000 pounds of bombs in their internal bomb bays. *Official USMC Photo*

A Marine F4U ripples off its entire load of HVARs as it dives on a ground target on Okinawa. The Marine fighters also attacked with iron bombs or napalm, and strafed ground targets with their six .50-caliber wing guns. The F4U was so successful in its role as a ground-support airplane that by this phase of the war the Marine Corps was decommissioning or converting many of its dive-bomber squadrons, none of which was ever deployed to Okinawa. *Official USMC Photo*

Indeed, Marine Air became almost wholly committed to XXIV Corps as it hit increasingly stiffer resistance in the south.

Beginning on April 7, MAG-31 and MAG-33 fighter pilots scored hundreds of aerial kills off Okinawa, particularly to the north, toward Japan. These included night kills by three Marine squadrons equipped with F6F-5N Hellcat night fighters based at Yontan. Also, six Marine F4U Corsair fighter squadrons were based aboard three fleet carriers, and they provided ground support and fleet cover. By April 1945, Marine Air was at the leading edge of technique and technology in support of modern combat operations across all three battle dimensions: land, sea, and air.

Guiding and controlling all 2d Marine Aircraft Wing day and night flight activity over and around Okinawa was a sophisticated array of radar-equipped air warning squadrons and landing force air support control units (like the one seen here). Night fighters could not find Japanese aerial intruders without guidance from ship- or ground-based radar controllers, and warning and control units and teams became particularly important as more and more Marine day fighters were deployed to throttle incessant lone sorties and mass attacks by kamikazes and conventional Japanese air units, especially against the invasion fleet and airfields. *Official USMC Photo*

The first IIIAC combat units to fight in southern Okinawa were the three 155mm gun battalions and three 155mm howitzer battalions of the 2d Provisional Artillery Group. This is a 1st 155mm Howitzer Battalion weapon. *Official USMC Photo*

8

THE FIGHT IN THE SOUTH

★ ★ ★ ★ ★

April 6–May 10, 1945

MARINES HEAD SOUTH

XXIV CORPS MET ITS FIRST REALLY STIFF OPPOSITION on the southern front on April 6. Thereafter, resistance became more violent and better organized to greater depths almost every step of the way. The defenses extended across the entire width of the island and to an undetermined depth. In fact, it was a concentric defense, complete and pervasive, centered on multiple rigdelines around the town of Shuri. Not apparent at the outset, but increasingly obvious with each passing day, the hard defenses could not and would not be carried by merely two infantry divisions supported by organic and corps artillery, nor even after XXIV Corps artillery was bolstered on April 7 by IIIAC's 2d Provisional Field Artillery Group (three 155mm gun battalions and three 155mm howitzer battalions), not to mention Marine Air based at Yontan and whatever carrier air the fleet had on hand for ground support duties.

Beginning on April 9, all four artillery battalions (three 105mm howitzer battalions and one 75mm pack howitzer battalion) of the 1st Marine Division's 11th Marines and two-thirds of a fresh army division were sent into the southern line, albeit with little effect. By April 14, XXIV Corps had killed nearly seven thousand Japanese, but it had barely made a dent in the defenses north of Shuri. A corps attack on April 19 supported by 27 artillery battalions and 375 aircraft sorties made negligible progress, then halted as the unperturbed Japanese troops moved back to their positions from secure underground shelters. The army divisions advanced only after the Japanese withdrew from the forward defensive line on the night of April 23–24 to a more integrated line to the rear.

On April 24, IIIAC was ordered to place one of its divisions in the Tenth Army reserve, and the 1st Marine Division was thus ordered to prepare to return to battle. (IIIAC's third division, the 2d, had been returned to Saipan to prepare for an amphibious assault near Okinawa that never took place.) On April 30, the 1st Marine Division advanced to replace

The lead elements of the 1st Marine Division relieved U.S. Army troops at the western end of the XXIV Corps line on April 30, 1945. *Official USMC Photo*

Colonel Kenneth Chappell (center), commanding officer of the 1st Marines, scans the regimental front on May 1 with Lieutenant Colonel James Murray (left), the commanding officer of 1/1. Murray was a highly regarded veteran who served in key staff positions at Guadalcanal and the central Solomons. *Official USMC Photo*

From the vantage point of the 1st Marines senior officers, looking southeast, the 1st Marine Division's main objectives can be viewed across the tops of several intermediate prominences interspersed with wide, flat, cultivated valleys. A raised highway cuts across the near vista from northeast to southwest. All the Marines know at this early juncture is that well-trained and veteran XXIV Corps troops got their noses bloodied on the way to these objectives. *Composited Official USMC Photos*

Heavy rains opened on May 1, as the 1st Marine Division assault units finished moving into the line and laying in battle supplies. Hardest hit in the valleys behind the lines were artillery emplacements and dirt roads that turned to muddy morasses by the passage of hundreds of vehicles charged with getting supplies and ammunition forward. *Official USMC Photo*

an army division on the right flank of the XXIV Corps zone, and that army division was ordered north to replace the 6th Marine Division so it could undertake a round of refitting followed by commitment to the southern battle.

The XXIV Corps infantry units the 1st Marine Division replaced at the edge of the Japanese southern defensive zone had been ground down to regiments little larger than battalions, and battalions little larger than companies. Dead ahead was the bulk of a well-trained Japanese infantry division holding a defensive sector the island command had just reorganized to higher levels of lethality. On the 1st Marine Division's first full day on the line, May 1, the weather turned cool and rainy, a state that would prevail into July.

✳ ✳ ✳

Front-line infantrymen gaze across the ground they are going to have to take in coming hours, days, and weeks. The problem they have, after a month of light combat, is coming to terms with the evidence that the Japanese ahead of them now are in large part well-led and experienced men whose confidence is no doubt high in the wake of the battering they have given to XXIV Corps troops who have already attempted to pacify these hills, ridges, and valleys.
Official USMC Photo

At nearly the last minute before the May 2 inaugural ground assault is launched, smoke rounds are placed on the valley floor to hide the leading files of Marines from view of the defenders. The .30-caliber medium machine gun has been set up on the forward brow of the high ground to provide overwatch and grazing fires in support of the advancing riflemen. Later, if all goes well, the medium machine guns will displace forward to strengthen the new front line.
Official USMC Photo

HARD CONTACT

The 1st Marine Division went into the offensive on May 2, the westernmost of three divisions in a coordinated Tenth Army attack. The 5th Marines was stymied at the outset, but adjacent 3/1 fell into a gap. The 1st Marines attempted to change direction to exploit the gap, and 3/1 advanced even farther in the rain before nightfall. On the other hand, I/1, on the division's right flank, faced fierce opposition, and portions of the battalion that were cut off had to withdraw, after which I/1 changed direction and won some new ground.

This baptismal day on the southern front was emblematic of the fighting that ensued. The Japanese made excellent use of broken ground and other natural cover, and the Marines were either stymied or fell into dead ground from which they could advance or from which they had to withdraw to maintain a cohesive line against the uncanny knack the defenders showed for mounting enfilade movements.

On May 3, the 5th Marines advanced more than 500 yards in its zone, but the 1st Marines was pinned down with heavy casualties, so the 5th had to pull back several hundred yards in places. There simply was no point at which the Marines could gain adequate leverage—the same scenario the replaced U.S. Army divisions had faced in their battle.

✵ ✵ ✵

continued on page 236

Scenes from a Battle:
April 2 and 3, 1945

Official USMC Photo

Official USMC Photo

Official USMC Photo

Official USMC Photo

Official USMC Photo

Official USMC Photo

Official USMC Photo

The quick use of armored amtracs during the chaotic counterlandings during the night of April 3–4 stemmed from the way they were deployed during the day. As the advance on land ground forward across waterways emptying into the sea on the 1st Marine Division right (west) flank, the armored amtracs provided direct flanking fire to suppress the Japanese opposing the crossing. When not in use, the armored amtracs hunkered down behind seawalls and other cover at the shoreline. Thus they were in perfect position to take on the Japanese landing barges. *Official USMC Photo*

The fighting on the 1st Marine Division front ran very hot on April 4 as the Marines simultaneously worked to root out stragglers and push ahead to objectives set out in briefings held before the counteroffensive kicked off. In this photo, Marines from 2/5 attempt to advance from a ridgeline against opposition that has stymied them for three days. They did manage to advance, but in the end they had to pull back to their initial line. *Official USMC Photo*

A 2/5 bazookaman takes aim at a target lower down. Few Japanese tanks challenged the destructive powers of the 2.36-inch (60mm) shape-charge rocket projectile fired by the bazooka, but many a Japanese fighting position succumbed to direct hits. *Official USMC Photo*

Continued from page 232
COUNTEROFFENSIVE

The Japanese had many thousands of first-line troops in reserve. These soldiers had been tied down defending beaches in southeastern Okinawa against landings that never took place. As the Japanese gained a finer sense of American tactics, it was put to the island commander that an offensive using these fresh, well-trained, and well-equipped troops might chasten the Americans and buy a great deal of time and flexibility. Some of the fresh troops were fed into the defensive sectors to make good the losses of weeks of bitter attritional warfare, but the bulk were held back to cover the suspect beaches or to serve as a mobile reserve. By May 2, a large portion of the fresh force had been fed into the Shuri sector to stiffen the defenses facing the 1st Marine Division. Ultimately, however, a number of senior Japanese officers won an argument in favor of launching a major tank-supported counteroffensive, including counterlandings behind American lines, that was to blunt the American offensive and perhaps throw it back.

Preceded by mass kamikaze attacks out of Japan that targeted rear areas on the island and logistical shipping offshore, the counteroffensive, including counterlandings on both coasts, began after dark on May 3. Artillery fire matched artillery fire at the front, while in the rear, Marines opened fire on Japanese troops coming ashore on the beach on which Company B, I/I, anchored the entire XXIV Corps line. This was not where the Japanese intended to land. Quick, cool reaction by the defenders and confusion among the mislanded attackers created conditions for a Marine victory. Many more Marines were fed into the fire-lit battle, LVT(A)s fighting in the sea sealed the battlefield, and

In the 1st Marines zone, a 37mm antitank gun from the regimental weapons company provides direct fire at a bunker lower down. The 37mm antitank guns typically fired armor-piercing rounds at fixed defensive emplacements or masonry buildings, and these often broke through even steel-reinforced concrete or stone via an accumulation of hits on the same spot. Okinawa was the last battle in which Marine Corps 37mm guns were ever used.
Official USMC Photo

A Marine infantry platoon advances up a draw through the smoke of a recent artillery or mortar barrage. Note the telltale signs that these Marines are veterans, or at least led by veterans: they are well spread out and wary in all directions, and each Marine seems ready to open fire at the least provocation.
Official USMC Photo

fresh troops hunted down infiltrators. Forewarned by this landing attempt, Marines quelled other attempts farther up the coast. Army troops also defended successfully on the eastern coast.

At dawn, behind an artillery curtain that never abated during the night and a rolling smoke barrage, the bulk of a battle-hardened Imperial Army infantry division crashed into a curtain of fire erected in front of two U.S. Army divisions by twelve 155mm and 8-inch gun and howitzer battalions and tag-team air attacks that mounted to 134 sorties by the day's end.

On May 4, the 1st Marine Division actually attacked in its zone despite the efforts of the Japanese to win through to the east, but the division was stalled several hundred yards short of its objective line.

Far from delaying an American victory, the ill-advised Japanese counteroffensive expended the largest reserve pool of seasoned fighters on the island, of whom nearly seven thousand were killed. But other good fighters had remained in their excellent defensive sectors, and they showed no sign of cracking appreciably in the face of inexorable pressure across the entire Tenth Army front. In less than a week on the Shuri front, 649 Marines became casualties.

The Japanese 32d Army, which oversaw the entire Okinawa defense, was in terrific shape even though it had suffered major setbacks in early May. At that time it had under its control in southern Okinawa at least one hundred thousand troops, many of whom could be rated good to excellent, most of them deployed in full-strength or nearly full-strength tactical units commanded by competent officers. Most units were well trained and retained their ability to maneuver competently. Many of 32d Army's best battalions had yet to see combat on the island, and there were enough full-strength battalions to rotate to the front lines as units

Official USMC Photo

IIIAC's Major General Roy Geiger (right) confers with Tenth Army's Lieutenant General Simon Bolivar Buckner Jr. Geiger, the fifth man and the first Marine ever to earn naval aviator wings, had commanded the 1st Marine Aircraft Wing at Guadalcanal, but he had been a corps commander since 1943 and had overseen the amphibious assaults at Bougainville and Guam before commanding all the Marines serving on Okinawa. *Official USMC Photo*

already there were weakened by intense combat. Japanese units on the front lines had the usual advantage of defenders, not least of which were long vistas across long, flat, open approaches, and the pick of commanding intermediate positions.

All this would change as the American infantry ground forward aided by their immense strength in artillery and highly mobile naval gunfire; alongside medium tanks deployed at the rate of one battalion per combat division; and via the use of air power, which for all practical purposes enjoyed total air supremacy more than 90 percent of the time and otherwise dominated the battlefield during every daylight hour.

Yes, 32d Army could inflict massive casualties on the U.S. Tenth Army. It could slow the American effort to pacify Okinawa, but it could not defeat it. Each and every day of battle, 32d Army would grow weaker and its combat components would become less able to turn in a top-notch defensive effort. The Japanese commanders had no reserve beyond the uncommitted troops already on Okinawa, but IIIAC alone still had access to the experienced and rested 6th Marine Division as well as the veteran and better-rested 2d Marine Division, which, even though it had been returned to the Marianas to prepare for the invasion of Japan, could return to Okinawa, in whole or in part, on relatively short notice. Japanese combat units not already arrayed on Okinawa would never be sent, for there was no Imperial Navy left to carry them there. The soldiers of 32d Army could bruise and delay Tenth Army but could never stop it, never defeat it, never deny it its tactical, operational, or strategic objectives.

OFFENSIVE RENEWED

Except for local actions (some quite fierce) to better their stance, most Marine front-line combat units stood down on May 5 and 6 to prepare for a IIIAC assault that was itself aimed at gaining good jump-off positions for a subsequent all-out Tenth Army offensive against the Japanese defenses centered on Shuri, a large hill town that straddled the IIIAC—XXIV Corps boundary. This all-out army-wide offensive was to begin on May 11.

May 5 was a day of relative peace on the 1st Marine Division front, but the troops remained alert and quite willing to draw blood if they could find targets on the Japanese front line. *Official USMC Photo*

A 1st Tank Battalion M4 provides fire support for an attack across rolling terrain on May 6. *Official USMC Photo*

Marines struggle to maintain their footing as they rush a wounded buddy along a dirt road just back of the front line. *Official USMC Photo*

Marines take turns resting and standing radio watch at a front-line company command post. *Official USMC Photo*

Infantry officers and forward observers of various stripes check out objectives and targets across the way. *Official USMC Photo*

On May 6, the 1st Marines mounted a frontal assault aimed at giving it a broader front for the corps attack set to begin the next day. Despite gallant efforts by the troops, the regiment's net gains for the day were zero. At the far left of the 5th Marines zone on May 6, 2/5 successfully advanced 200 yards to tie in with an army battalion across the corps boundary. Nevertheless an effort by the rest of the regiment to close on the fiercely defended Awacha Pocket made only the slightest gains despite help from four artillery battalions, naval gunfire, and close air support.

Hampered by heavy rain but bolstered by massive artillery, air, rocket, and naval gunfire support, the 1st and 5th Marines jumped off on May 7 several hours later than planned. Both regiments were immediately stymied by steadfast defenders all across their fronts. At one point, 2/1 fought its way to the top of a hill that dominated the regimental front, but it had to give up the feature when a large Japanese force massed for a counterattack. In the center of the adjacent sector, where the Japanese remained dug into the Awacha Pocket, 1/5 gained 200 to 300 yards, but 2/5, on the regimental left, and 3/5, on the right, gained a only few yards here and there. Also on May 7, the 6th Marine Division's 22d Marines began to move toward the southern line.

On May 8 1/22 and 3/22 replaced the 7th Marines on the far right (west) of the Tenth Army front line. Directly ahead of the 22d Marines was the wide Asa Kawa estuary, which for a week the 7th Marines had been unable to cross in the face of defiant Japanese resistance. During the day, also, IIIAC resumed full operational control of both Marine divisions.

Rain stalled the May 8 assault all across the IIIAC front, but Marines had a rewarding enough day mopping up Japanese bunkers, pillboxes, and caves within immediate reach. To suppress Japanese emplacements farther out, two 75mm pack howitzer batteries were man-handled to the front lines, one each for the 1st and 5th Marines.

On May 9, the 22d Marines patrolled its sector at the far right of the IIIAC line, more to familiarize itself with battlefield conditions than to learn anything that hadn't been passed along

continued on page 244

In its May 7 attack, 2/1 received direct fire support from the regimental weapons company's two M7 assault guns. Seen here, an assault gun crew goes through the drill of firing a 105mm round at a directly observable target: load, fire, and make way for the expended shell casing to drop from the breech. *Official USMC Photos*

Marine riflemen and a bazooka team search for targets during a firefight with Japanese troops directly across the way. *Official USMC Photo*

A pair of demotions assaultmen wait to see what happens after tossing a white phosphorus grenade into a Japanese-manned burrow. So far, one dead Japanese soldier lies at the feet of the Marine to the right. *Official USMC Photo*

Their planned assault called on account of rain, many 1st Marine Division troops spent May 8 taking down Japanese defenses within easy reach of their front-line positions. Seen here, Marine infantrymen flinch just as a satchel charge detonates inside a burrow. *Official USMC Photo*

A .30-caliber light machine gun team puts out a steady stream of suppressive fire against a patch of Japanese-held terrain.
Official USMC Photo

A sniper team—sniper and observer—peer at a smoke-shrouded hillside in the hope that Japanese troops will flee an artillery barrage. *Official USMC Photo*

Continued from page 240

when the regiment moved in. To the east, the 1st Marine Division attacked through heavy rain. Tanks were able to support drives in some areas, and where they did, 1st Division troops gained as many as 300 yards, which helped straighten the overall division line. Late in the day, the 7th Marines moved from the rear to positions from which it would squeeze between the 1st Marines, on the 1st Marine Division right, and the 5th Marines, on the IIIAC far left.

Unbeknownst to the Marines, 32d Army also had been swapping units into and out of the line facing IIIAC; by the wee hours of May 10, Marines faced mostly fresh, full-strength combat battalions, several of which made moves to infiltrate the 5th Marines zone. Between 0200 and 0300 hours on May 10, 1/5 beat off two direct assaults in hand-to-hand fighting that resulted in sixty Japanese corpses being left behind.

On May 10, 1st Marine Division again attacked in the rain against stiff opposition, most notably on the left, where tanks sent to support the 5th Marines once again bogged down on muddy

continued on page 250

Levitating a 75mm pack howitzer up a steep hillside is backbreaking work, but it is well worth the effort in terms of the damage two 75mm batteries will be able to do once they are emplaced directly on the 1st and 5th Marines front lines. *Official USMC Photo*

All manner of supplies and ammunition had to be ported up steep, muddy hillsides on the backs of Marines. *Official USMC Photo*

Casualty evacuation aboard a 1st Tank Battalion M4. *Official USMC Photo*

On May 9 the 1st Marine Division achieved notable results in several places as the 1st and 5th Marines once again attempted to reach the line from which the Tenth Army offensive was to jump off on May 11. Tanks were especially valuable where they could operate, but all across the division front, Marines on foot, using all manner of portable weapons, gave their utmost to crack the stubborn Japanese defenses, with or without tank support.
Official USMC Photos

When 2/5 came under attack on the night of May 9–10, Marines launched flares to locate Japanese units that might be on the move to reinforce or broaden the assault. *Official USMC Photo*

As the 1st Marine Division attack resumes, engineers attempt to locate mines along a roadway recently captured from the Japanese. Hundreds of mines were located and harvested by such efforts, but by no means all of them. *Official USMC Photo*

Scenes from a Battle:
May 10, 1945

Official USMC Photos

At length on May 10, the 5th Marines swept into a draw dubbed Death Valley, because it is reputed that 125 Marines were killed or wounded to take it. Here, a BAR-man steels himself for a dash to join Marines farther along who maintain a tenuous grip on this hard-won piece of ground. *Official USMC Photo*

Marines take cover in Death Valley as their positions are swept by heavy fire from heights on two sides. *Official USMC Photo*

Continued from page 244

roads. In short order, 1/5 was pinned by intense fire, and it remained in place, taking a pummeling, until it could at last pull back at 1700 hours under cover of a smoke barrage. On the other hand, 2/5 eventually got tank support, and it conquered its share of the particularly nettlesome Awacha Pocket. Nearby, a severely battered 3/5 took its objective, a fireswept draw Marines had dubbed Death Valley for very good reason. In the 7th Marines zone, where 3/7 was stumped by heavy fire as soon as it jumped off, 1/7 made a good deal of progress but was then pummeled senseless and ultimately had to withdraw because 1/5, adjacent to the left, had been held up and the Japanese had taken advantage of the gap between the regiments to work 1/7 over quite brutally. On the 1st Marine Division right, the 1st Marines ultimately took possession of a low ridge overlooking an important lateral road, but the assault troops were driven to ground by heavy machine-gun fire and thus could not quite cross the road.

In the new 6th Marine Division zone, the 6th Engineer Battalion needed to throw a prebuilt footbridge across the Asa Kawa estuary; otherwise the 22d Marines would remain penned in by this stretch of deep water. This was accomplished at 0300 hours on May 10, and two companies each from 1/22 and 3/22 immediately crossed to the southern bank to create and defend a bridgehead. At 0530 hours, a pair of Japanese sappers on a suicide mission destroyed the southern end of the footbridge with a satchel charge. In response to a contingency for which there was a plan, Marine engineers accompanying the assault battalions breached the continuous concrete seawall with their own high explosives, and soon amtracs filled with troops and supplies were plying a route back and forth across the mouth of the Asa Kawa. Meantime, 1/22 and 3/22 kicked off their planned assault through smoke and fog to a depth of 150 yards. The advance stalled there in the face of heavy defensive fires that just got heavier for hours. Nevertheless, aggressive tactics by 1/22 and 3/22 eventually won through to a depth of 350 yards in some places. Marine tanks and other supporting arms too large or too heavy for transport aboard amtracs remained on the Asa Kawa's northern bank until after a Bailey bridge was thrown in six hours during the night of May 10–11.

Although IIIAC's four front-line regiments had fallen short of all their objectives in five days of heavy fighting in bad weather, there was no thought given to delaying the two-corps assault Tenth Army planned to open on the morning of May 11, 1945.

Reproduced in countless versions, from oil paintings to T-shirts to commemorative plates to bronze statuettes, this timeless photo, which perfectly captures the essence of the combat infantryman, has touched the hearts and honed the honor of three generations of United States Marines. Here, Corporal Paul Ison, a twenty-eight-year-old autoworker turned into a demolitions assaultman serving with Company L, 3/5, runs for his life across 75 fireswept yards of Death Valley to bring a load of explosive charges he and his fellow assaultmen will use to clear the southern verges of Death Valley and thus secure this dangerous piece of ground once and for all.
Official USMC Photo

U.S. Marine Corps/National Archives

9

OVER THE HILLS AND INTO THE CITIES

May 11–June 22, 1945

ATTRITION

FROM THE BEGINNING OF THE TENTH ARMY OFFENSIVE on May 11, despite interesting tactical embellishments, the battle to win Okinawa settled down to become a test of attritional theories, one based on attack and the other based on defense. For two terrible weeks, IIIAC remained locked in an expensive, heart-rending battle of attrition for a distant objective: Shuri, the highest point on a faraway ridgeline walling in the far side of a broad valley. The valley was interspersed and further dominated by a jumble of intervening ridges and stand-alone prominences, on each of which the defenders had placed at least some competent to excellent combat troops bolstered by an uncanny ability to dig virtually invisible emplacements deep into the earth and rock. Elsewhere during the long, bloody Pacific offensive, Marine divisions had suffered more grievous blood baths in shorter periods than the damnable attrition to which they were subjected before Shuri, but there would still be so much of Okinawa left to take after Shuri fell—as inevitably it must—that some commanders became cautious of the losses and, as often as they could, wielded their troops like scalpels rather than the otherwise obligatory sledgehammers of Tarawa, Peleliu, and Iwo Jima. But such finesse did not often match the ground or the mood of the defenders, so blunt-force trauma—expensive and heart-rending—was the technique to which most delicate plans ultimately devolved.

Emblematic of the entire state of combat throughout the period was the hyperintense battle between May 13 and May 19 for three interlocked defensive sectors on adjacent hill masses known *continued on page 257*

continued on page 257

A 105mm howitzer helps pummel Japanese positions on the night of May 11, 1945. *Official USMC Photo*

Marine riflemen wait for survivors to vault from a cave that is being worked over by a flame tank. *Official USMC Photo*

A medium machine gun squad hauls its gear forward on May 11 in the wake of advancing riflemen. *Official USMC Photo*

The Sugar Loaf

A platoon leader points out the day's objectives as the Marines prepare to jump off against the Sugar Loaf and nearby hill complexes. *Official USMC Photo*

An assault on the Sugar Loaf has just jumped off. This early in the battle, the vegetation is still in good shape. *Official USMC Photo*

One large feature of the days-long assault in the Sugar Loaf area was the constant flow of casualties. Whole Marine infantry battalions were bled dry in the attritional battle. *Official USMC Photo*

As riflemen cling to what little cover they can find on this denuded hillside, a bazooka team prepares to fire on a Japanese position. If the Japanese position is destroyed, the infantry will attempt to move ahead even though it is likely Japanese manning covering positions will try to stop them. *Official USMC Photo*

The key to taking the Sugar Loaf and adjacent hills was for the infantry to advance to open ground, thus providing viable avenues of approach for Marine medium tanks, which pretty much overwhelmed the rest of the fraying defenses. Note that contrary to hard lessons turned into doctrine, these medium tanks are advancing without the usual close-in infantry support. *Official USMC Photo*

This longitudinal view of the Sugar Loaf, taken during the final attack by 6th Tank Battalion M4s, shows how relatively small the defiantly defended feature is. *Official USMC Photo*

A 1/29 rifle platoon uses a tank for cover as it advances on May 17 along a railroad cut toward Shuri. *Official USMC Photo*

A tank tests the waters as infantrymen prepare for an assault over open ground. *Official USMC Photo*

Continued from page 253

as Sugar Loaf Hill, The Horse Shoe, and the Half Moon. On these hills, whole battalions of the 22d and 29th Marines ground themselves to dust in toe-to-toe fighting in which neither side cut the other any slack whatsoever. And even after these three hills fell, at enormous human expense to both sides, Shuri itself remained at the far side of yet another jumble of expertly defended, vigorously assaulted hills and draws in which the blunt questions and answers regarding ownership generated even longer casualty rolls.

✳ ✳ ✳

continued on page 262

A front-line corpsman treats a wounded front-line Marine. Plasma or whole blood were routinely administered to fight shock as well as to replace blood volume. *Official USMC Photo*

An officer consoles a grief-stricken Marine whose closest friend has just died on the road to Shuri. *Official USMC Photo*

First Marine Division infantry units mount all-out assaults on May 21 against Wana Ridge and Wana Draw, one of the last stoutly defended zones guarding Shuri.
Official USMC Photos

This 81mm mortar was silenced by a direct hit on May 23. One crewman was killed and two were wounded, a low toll given the explosive power that might have been unleashed if the ammunition supply had been detonated. *Official USMC Photo*

Below: Covered by a kamikaze strike on the invasion fleet undertaken by hundreds of aircraft on the night of May 24–25, a dozen obsolete Imperial Navy medium bombers attempted to crash-land on Yontan Airfield to deliver 120 commandos on a suicide mission to disrupt air operations. Eleven of the troop-filled aircraft were shot down, but the last made a safe wheels-up landing, and its complement of 10 commandos fought a mixed bag of surprised groundcrew, aircrew, and pilots in the dark until all of the intruders had been killed. Several American aircraft were disabled or destroyed, two Americans were killed, and eighteen Americans were wounded, some no doubt victims of indiscriminate defensive gunfire. *Official USMC Photos*

Surprised, wary, and ultimately happy Marines advance safely into formerly contested ground on the Shuri front in the wake of the Japanese disengagement. Scores of Japanese dead littered the ground first overrun by 1st Marine Division patrols, and many hundreds were ultimately discovered in makeshift hospitals set up inside many of the caves. Hundreds of wounded Japanese were euthanized or simply left to die by their own doctors and medics when the 32d Army's casualty evacuation plan broke down at the height of the withdrawal. *Official USMC Photo*

Lieutenant Colonel Richard Ross Jr., the commanding officer of 3/1, plants the 1st Marine Division's national colors atop the ruins of Shuri Castle on May 30, 1945. These same colors flew over Cape Gloucester and Peleliu and were personally entrusted to Ross by the division commander. *Official USMC Photo*

The road to Naha. The 6th Marine Division's 4th and 22d Marines close on Okinawa's capital city on the far right of the Tenth Army front. *Official USMC Photo*

Below: In a classic attack into urban terrain, the city or town is first isolated around its periphery—to deny the defenders access to outside resources and lines of retreat. Then the cityscape is typically "prepped" with artillery fire and air attacks. Naha could not be surrounded; the 6th Marine Division could only approach the city from the northeast because wide bodies of water isolated the city to the north and west. The realities of terrain led to the only viable plan of attack, a direct frontal assault from open terrain into dense cityscape. *Official USMC Photos*

Continued from page 257

NAHA

Okinawa's capital city, Naha, stood on the island's western coast, directly in the path of the 6th Marine Division's 22d Marines and overlapping into the zone of the 4th Marines. Naha was a full-fledged city, a dense concrete and masonry maze of multistory buildings on paths, streets, and boulevards meandering off in every direction. It was by far the largest urban area Marines faced in the Pacific War.

The Marine Corps as a whole had done very little to prepare its combat arms for urban warfare, and none had taken place until mid-1944, when combat units were obliged to secure several towns in the Marianas, on Saipan, Tinian, and Guam. The Marines made do and won through, reinventing age-old tactics as they went. On Guam, the 1st Marine Brigade, which was ultimately expanded to become 6th Marine Division, took part in several urban battles, and this led the commanding general to subject his troops to actually training

for urban combat in time to move out to Okinawa. No one could have guessed that these trained troops would be matched up to undertake the largest urban battle in Marine Corps history to that time.

The 6th Marine Division reached the eastern outskirts of Naha on May 25, at which point Japanese defenders holding numerous houses and burial vaults made it abundantly clear that the city was to be aggressively defended. The city was indeed aggressively defended at the outset, and fighting to take possession of it was amply complicated by a 60-foot-wide canal that effectively bifurcated the battlefield and thus obligated the 6th Marine Division to fight two battles, one with the 4th Marines

continued on page 270

Built-up areas are extremely difficult for men on the ground to picture. Buildings and hills often impede vistas, and the only open ground is often streets, roads, and parks, which defenders (whose vision also is restricted) tend to stake out to get clear shots at attackers, who must cross them sooner or later. Beginning in late 1943 at Cape Gloucester, and weather permitting, Marine combat forces usually employed aerial observers to call in battlefield data from beyond the sight of troops on the ground. Aerial observers typically directed air, artillery, and naval gunfire missions. *Official USMC Photo*

On the ground itself, extreme battle is often waged for possession of hills within the city or the top floors of the highest buildings in a neighborhood. In an urban setting, a hill, a tall building, or a church steeple is a perfect spot for a sniper or an artillery forward observer, and such "high ground" naturally attracts the attention—and fire—of men at ground level. Numerous techniques can be employed to neutralize "high ground," but in the end it requires physical possession to really neutralize it. Then it can be used by the winning side's snipers and forward observers. *Official USMC Photos*

Armor is a mixed blessing in urban terrain. A tank can withstand all manner of fire while it stands off—or wades right in—to demolish buildings in the path of assaulting infantry, but it takes a lot of troops to defend a buttoned-up tank whose crew has extremely limited vistas and is thus prone to retreat unless aggressively protected. Moreover, tanks can be heard a long way off, and they tend to attract great volumes of defensive fire that tends to drive accompanying infantry to cover. *Official USMC Photo*

The nature of even undisturbed urban terrain—block after block of individual buildings composed of one, two, or many levels of rooms separated by walls composed of everything from wood lathe to steel-reinforced concrete—tends to balkanize tactical units to their lowest common denominators, squads or fire teams isolated from any form of higher command or, quite often, access to supporting arms. Leadership is often impossible to impose or maintain even at the squad level, and the raw exigencies of survival tend to send troops scattering to the winds far from the view of comrades, not to mention troop leaders and commanders. Flames and rubble further break up unit cohesion as well as provide defenders with serendipitous tools that multiply the inherent benefits of trying to hold urban terrain. *Official USMC Photo*

Even when company commanders, platoon leaders, and squad leaders have access to reliable radios, conversation can be impeded by loud noises echoing off hard surfaces or by physical barriers. Results can fall short of needs due to misunderstandings caused by such noise and visual barriers. Fortunately, by 1945, Marine infantry squads were organized into three four-man fire teams, each built around a Browning automatic rifle (BAR). Fire team leaders in the 6th Marine Division were especially well trained to cope with being on their own, without benefit of supervision from even their squad leaders. *Official USMC Photo*

In Naha, direct-fire weapons, such as the 37mm antitank gun or the 2.36-inch bazooka, were extremely useful where walls and doors needed to be taken down. Mortars and artillery are less reliable—as well as a danger to friendly troops—unless their fire can be closely observed and minutely controlled. *Official USMC Photos*

Automatic weapons are always useful in an urban setting. They can be used to keep defenders' heads down as attackers rush across open spaces, and they can literally chip away at defenses. They do tend to draw a great deal of attention from defenders, so they need to be well shielded.
Official USMC Photo

Cover is what it is in an urban setting. Even a flimsy wall is good cover if a soldier is able to move along one side without being seen from the other. But many nonpenetrating hits by bullets or even artillery, mortars, antitank guns, and tank guns are deadly to troops holed up or traversing an area behind a wall. Enough firepower over a long enough time can drive defenders from even excellent cover, and the kinetic energy of high-velocity hits on one side of a masonry wall can result in casualties on the other side through spalling. Flying debris, even tiny shards that carom around in the open, but especially those that carom within confined spaces, can be as deadly as bullets or shrapnel.
Official USMC Photos

Rubble is a two-edge sword. Blowing a building apart can cause death or severe injury to defenders as well as flatten out city vistas (which itself cuts both ways), but it also creates hazards for attackers by offering uncountable opportunities for defenders to find cover the human eye cannot discern among the chaos of dust-shrouded, piled-up rubble. There is no good way to cope with rubble and ruins in embattled urban settings; they are simply universal factors to which attackers and defenders alike need to adapt. *Official USMC Photos*

This herd of loping infantrymen is the logo for urban combat. These Marines needed to move, but is it safe? How much looking around can they do before a hidden defender spots them? There are so many possibilities for hunter and hunted that it's often impossible to say which is which. In the end, achieving victory requires that men armored in cloth shirts cross sharply restricted, easily defined open areas the opposition might as easily have staked out as not. *Official USMC Photo*

Optimally, large patches of urban terrain can be preliminarily cleared by the swift advance of footborne infantry supported by tanks. Eventually, however, terrain cleared so swiftly must be painstakingly combed on foot to locate booby traps and mines as well as to flush out defenders who have been trapped by the swift advance or intentionally left behind to terrorize rear-echelon troops and headquarters. *Official USMC Photo*

This is what veteran, battle-aware street fighters look like. The nearest Marine walks in a stoop from which he can drop to the ground and return fire in a heartbeat. The Marine directly behind him reflexively checks an opening in his cover even though at least two Marines (the automatic rifleman and the photographer) have already safely passed it. *Official USMC Photo*

Marines attempt to overcome a feature known as Cemetery Ridge on June 1.
Official USMC Photo

Marines of 2/22 observe artillery fire from a hilltop trench south of Naha.
Official USMC Photo

Naha Airdrome fell to 3/4 and supporting tanks following a two-day battle on June 4 and 5. *Official USMC Photo*

Continued from page 263

(relieved by the 29th Marines on May 28) to the east and the other with the 22d Marines to the west.

Unbeknownst to the Marine urban combatants, 32d Army, on May 26, ordered most of the defenders to withdraw from Naha and adjacent areas. Only a tough rearguard fight would be offered to slow the Americans. The city was all but completely in Marine hands by the late afternoon of May 29, following an unprecedented 600-yard advance that day by the 29th Marines.

END GAME

On May 26, 32d Army ordered most units in contact with Tenth Army to prepare to undertake a general withdrawal on May 28 to final defensive positions farther south. Several powerful units already set in around Shuri, along with reinforcements, were ordered to screen the withdrawal and slow the pursuit the Americans were bound to push out from their lines. Thus Shuri and its defensive keystone, Shuri Castle, did not fall into 1st Marine Division hands until May 29, but fall they did, at which point the Japanese rearguard defensive effort in adjacent areas collapsed. In turn, Tenth Army opened what all hands hoped would be the final drive to wrest the remainder of Okinawa. The Japanese gave ground when they had no troops to hold it, but they also fought with their typical stoic effectiveness wherever they stood a chance of delaying the inevitable American victory, and that they did, day after bloody day.

IIIAC had a large, ample pool of replacements, covering all specialties. These fillers were employed as logistical laborers until needed in the combat battalions. Attrition was

As soon as they could get a little time to themselves, Marines from 3/4 bathe in a water-filled shell crater on Naha Airdrome. This might be their first real bath in a month.
Official USMC Photo

high among all the American divisions—ultimately 11,147 replacements would be fed into Marine units alone on Okinawa. But when a Japanese veteran was killed, he could not be replaced, except at the expense of some other unit. Yet in almost every phase of the battle, even the least competent Japanese soldiers fought to the last when they were cornered. This last truth is what truly shaped the campaign to wrest the shrinking remainder of southern Okinawa from Japanese hands.

Deadly combinations of spirited infantry assaults, overwhelming artillery and naval gunfire support, along with ample air support, were played like a piano in fighting the remainder of the campaign. The concentric lines of defense built and held by the Japanese never got easier to reduce, but inexorably the quality and number of the troops holding them shifted downward, and they did fall, one after the other.

The battle lines crawled south over weeks, for which American and Japanese men died in their hundreds and thousands.

The 2d Marine Division's 8th Marines took part in several landings on islands to the northwest of Okinawa, beginning on June 3. The regiment ultimately went ashore on Okinawa to serve with the 1st Marine Division, beginning on June 17, for the final assaults of the campaign.

An interesting footnote to Marine Corps history came about on June 18 when the Tenth Army commander, Lieutenant General Simon Bolivar Buckner Jr., was shot dead in the 8th Marines line while reconnoitering the front. The next-senior general officer on the scene was Marine Major General Roy Geiger, the IIIAC commanding general. Geiger,

Marines blow a cave near Naha. *Official USMC Photo*

an aviator who had commanded the 1st Marine Aircraft Wing at Guadalcanal, I Marine Amphibious Corps at Bougainville, and IIIAC at Guam and Okinawa, was spot-promoted to lieutenant general to become the first and only Marine and the first and only naval aviator—perhaps the first and only aviator—ever to command an American field army in the field.

The Japanese defenses were all but overwhelmed by June 16, and the 32d Army commanding general accepted that the end was near. On June 19, he dissolved his staff and ordered all available troops to go over to guerrilla operations. On June 21, organized resistance ended in the 6th Marine Division zone, which encompassed the southern shore of the island. By then, Japanese troops were surrendering in the hundreds. The 1st Marine Division mounted its final attacks of the campaign, also on June 21, and reported by nightfall that all its objectives had been secured. XXIV Corps made similar announcements. It thus fell to General Geiger to declare Okinawa secure following a bloody, grinding eighty-two-day battle. The final official flag-raising ceremony on a Pacific War battlefield took place at the Tenth Army headquarters at 1000 hours on June 22, 1945.

A blade tank clears the way for gun tanks during the pursuit of Japanese forces in southern Okinawa. Only a handful of the useful blade tanks were assigned to each tank battalion, and none before 1945. *Official USMC Photo*

A Marine F4U (upper right of photo) smears napalm across a previously undisturbed ridge in southern Okinawa. *Official USMC Photo*

Groundcrewmen load plastic bags of water into padded canisters that will be dropped to front-line troops racing to catch up with the receding 32d Army. *Official USMC Photo*

A Marine TBM makes a low-level supply drop to Marines just behind the front line. *Official USMC Photo*

A wounded Marine is eased aboard an OY observation plane operating from a stretch of level roadway just behind the front line. Such aerial evacuations by Marine light planes first took place on Okinawa. *Official USMC Photo*

The battle for Okinawa had been among the most brutal of the Pacific War. The U.S. Navy suffered its greatest casualties for a single engagement. More than 12,000 Americans from all services were killed or missing in action, and a further 50,000 were wounded. An estimated 130,000 Japanese combatants were killed during the battle, and 10,755 were captured. Civilian losses were pegged at approximately 42,000 killed or wounded.

At the close of the battle, all hands turned to, to begin preparations for the invasion of Kyushu. Already, army air forces bomber groups that had been in Europe on VE Day were on their way to join hundreds of Marine and army air forces warplanes already operating

Marines risk their lives alongside a fireswept roadway to get ammunition to their unit. *Official USMC Photo*

During fighting on June 12 around Hill 69, a demolitions assaultman prepares to swing a 24-pound satchel charge through the entrance of a cave presumably occupied by Japanese troops. *Official USMC Photo*

This Marine rifleman shot and killed this Japanese army nurse on June 12 as she made her way off embattled Hill 69 in the company of a doctor and a medic, who also were killed. The nurse's haversack contained two hand grenades and rifle ammunition.
Official USMC Photo

During clearing operations on June 14, the Marine on the left prepares to drop a smoke grenade into the mouth of an occupied cave. The idea is to induce the occupants to surrender rather than go down fighting.
Official USMC Photo

A 2/29 flamethrower assaultman lays a stream of flame on a cave during clearing operations on Oroku Peninsula. *Official USMC Photo*

A 6th Tank Battalion tank retriever, built on a turretless M4 body, tows a damaged tank to the rear. Often as not, tank retriever crews could perform engine repairs and resolve other problems in the field. *Official USMC Photo*

Japan's 32nd Army was only days away from utter collapse, but the rate of casualties incurred in southern Okinawa never abated. *Official USMC Photo*

from Okinawa's airfields (as well as *thousands* of American, British, and Canadian carrier-based aircraft) in the massive, unrelenting aerial bombardment that was to lay waste to the southernmost Japanese home island, Kyushu, before a contemplated October invasion was set in motion.

Who could have known on June 22, 1945, that only some six weeks separated America's Pacific Warriors from the kindling of two suns in the skies over Hiroshima and Nagasaki that would send the vast majority home to the peace so many thousands of their brave comrades had died to secure.

The 8th Marines hikes south across Naha Airdrome on June 16 to join the battle as part of the 1st Marine Division. *Official USMC Photo*

Voluntary surrenders picked up appreciably as the last active units of 32d Army were squeezed toward Okinawa's southern tip. The Marine checking the Japanese soldier's papers is armed with a .45-caliber M3 submachine gun, known as a grease gun because of its silhouette. The M3 was a cheap substitute for the beautifully engineered Thompson submachine gun. Very few M3s reached Marine units through official channels during the Pacific War. *Official USMC Photo*

Marines of 2/22 salute as they unfurl the national colors on the beach beside the battalion's final objective. The impromptu flag-raising was held in honor of Lieutenant Colonel Horatio Woodhouse Jr., who was killed while directing these troops in the front line on May 30. *Official USMC Photo*

In only a few years, all of America's Pacific Warriors will be gone, known only by history but kept near in the hearts of their children and grandchildren, on unto generations unborn. *Official USMC Photo*

'Til the last landing's made
And we stand unafraid
On a shore no mortal has seen,
'Til the last bugle call
Sounds Taps for us all,
It's Semper Fidelis, Marine.

BIBLIOGRAPHY

Blakeney, Jane. *Heroes: U.S. Marine Corps, 1861–1955.* Blakeney Publishing, 1956.

Frank, Benis M., and Henry I. Shaw, Jr. *Victory and Occupation.* Vol. V, *History of U.S. Marine Corps Operations in World War II.* Washington, D.C.: U.S. States Marine Corps, 1968.

Garand, George W., and Truman R. Strobridge. *Western Pacific Operations.* Vol. IV, *History of U.S. Marine Corps Operations in World War II.* Washington, D.C.: U.S. States Marine Corps, 1971.

Hammel, Eric. *Air War Pacific: Chronology, America's Air War Against Japan in East Asia and the Pacific, 1941–1945.* Pacifica, Calif.: Pacifica Press, 1998.

———. *Pacific Warriors: The U.S. Marines in World War II, A Pictorial Tribute.* St. Paul: Zenith Press, 2005.

Mondey, David. *Concise Guide to American Aircraft of World War II.* London: Temple Press, 1982.

———. *Concise Guide to Axis Aircraft of World War II.* London: Temple Press, 1984.

Nalty, Bernard C. *The Right to Fight: African-American Marines in World War II.* Washington, D.C.: Marine Corps Historical Center, 1995.

Newcomb, Richard F. *Iwo Jima.* New York: Holt, Rinehart & Winston, 1965.

Olynyk, Frank J. *USMC Credits for the Destruction of Enemy Aircraft in Air-to-Air Combat, World War 2.* Aurora, Ohio: Frank J. Olynyk, 1981.

Ross, Bill D. *Iwo Jima: Legacy of Valor.* New York: Vanguard Press, 1985.

Shaw, Henry I. Jr., Bernard C. Nalty, and Edwin T. Turnbladh. *Central Pacific Drive.* Vol. III, *History of U.S. Marine Corps Operations in World War II.* Washington, D.C.: United States Marine Corps, 1966.

Sherrod, Robert. *History of Marine Corps Aviation in World War II.* San Rafael, Calif.: Presidio Press, 1980.

Toland, John. *The Rising Sun: The Decline and Fall of the Japanese Empire, 1936–1945.* New York: Random House, 1970.

Williams, Mary H. *Chronology, 1941–1945: United States Army in World War II.* Washington, D.C.: Office of the Chief of Military History, 1960.

INDEX